THE INCOMPARABLE Christ

Other books by the same author:

Reflections on the Baptism in the Holy Spirit
Reflections on the Gifts of the Spirit
Reflections on a Song of Love (1 Cor 13)
A Trumpet Call to Women
Consider Him
Battle for the Body
The Clash of Tongues: with Glimpses of Revival

For early publication:

Gospel Vignettes
Reflections from Abraham

In course of preparation:

Christian Fundamentals
Pioneers of the Spiritual Way
Reflections on Moses

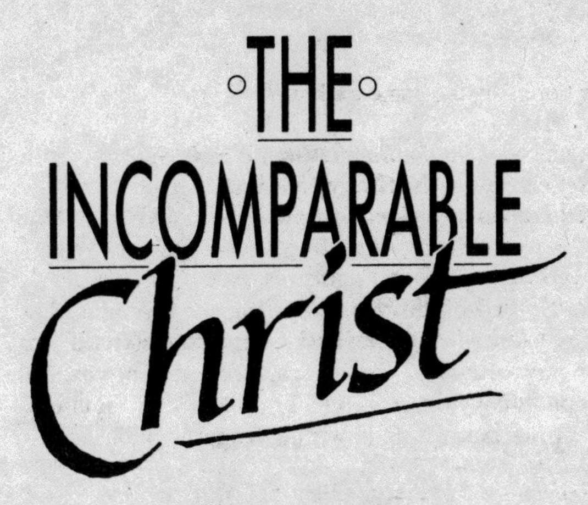

Hugh B. Black

NEW DAWN BOOKS
GREENOCK, SCOTLAND

First published 1989 by
NEW DAWN BOOKS
27 Denholm Street, Greenock PA16 8RH, Scotland

ISBN 1 870944 07 0

Most of the author's biblical references are to the
Revised Version.

Cover photo: Craig Richardson

Production and printing in England for
NEW DAWN BOOKS
27 Denholm Street, Greenock PA16 8RH, Scotland by
Nuprint Ltd, 30b Station Road, Harpenden, Herts AL5 4SE.

Dedication

To my father, who was a man of God and a great lover of the gospel. Though not a platform speaker, he was a skilful fisher of men. He died almost sixty years ago and yet his memory has remained vivid through a lifetime. I remember him as clearly as though he had died last night. His influence has been life-long.

Acknowledgements

I am grateful to all of those who continue to encourage me to write; to my wife Isobel and to my daughter Alison for editorial assistance; to Miss Pauline Anderson, Mr Alistair Duff, Miss Jennifer Jack and Mr George Marshall for proof reading and general advice; and to Alison and Miss Irene Morrison for laborious work in processing the book.

My thanks are also due to the authors and publishers whose works have been quoted, some of whom I would particularly like to mention.

Josh McDowell's *Evidence that Demands a Verdict* proved to be a veritable gold mine relative to Old Testament prophecies fulfilled in Christ and to evidence of His resurrection (and, I noticed, to a wide variety of other subjects as well). Herbert Lockyer's *All the Messianic Prophecies of the Bible* also proved useful.

Antero Korhonen's *Lord, I Am in Agony*, to whose unpublished translation in English by Willie Kinnaird I had access, throws unusual light on the early Christians' attitude to death. Otto Borchert's *The Original Jesus* gave valuable insights into the Jews' expectations regarding the Messiah as did Fruchtenbaum's *Jesus Was a Jew*.

Dean Farrar's *Life of Christ* has long been a favourite work. His view of Judas has been helpful.

Finally, I am indebted to F. W. Myers for his haunting lines on Paul, to the authors known and unknown of 'One Solitary Life,' 'The Incomparable Christ,' and 'Ecce Homo.'

I have been able to bring these last three prose poems, which I have long loved, together in one book.

To all, my appreciation and thanks.

Contents

Foreword

The charismatic renewal that began in the 1960's introduced a new awareness of the Person and Power of the Holy Spirit into mainline Protestant and Catholic churches. This evoked a flood of literature to meet an increasing demand for explanation of new phenomena hitherto unexperienced. Scotland had a dearth of writers capable of drawing from personal experience and providing positive teaching. One notable exception is Hugh Black. His personal experience has been forged in the crucible of opposition, persecution and ridicule, and has been drawn from a widespread ministry spanning four decades.

My first introduction to Mr Black came through his books, *Reflections on the Baptism in the Holy Spirit*, *Reflections on the Gifts of the Spirit* and *Battle for the Body*. My ten years as a missionary amongst Moslems in the Middle East had opened my eyes and spirit to the real nature of spiritual warfare. The Baptism of the Holy Spirit therefore was not only a most welcome experience but the vital source of the only power capable of overcoming the insidious power of evil in whatever form it assumed or situation it exploited. It presented no difficulty for me therefore to identify with and draw encouragement from Mr Black's writings. What distinguished his writings from the many books I had read which were dedicated to expounding the work of the Holy Spirit was his underlying and overall message of holiness. The reader is left in no doubt that 'purity is the key to power.' When I recently met Mr Black I found an immediate spiritual affinity which only confirmed my expectations.

In this his first book addressed specifically to the revelation of Christ in the Gospel, Mr Black weaves for us a beautiful tapestry portraying the incomparable Christ in all His glorious splendour and humility. To assume however that this magnificent and graphic picture is presented simply to evoke admiration of the Eternal Christ is to misconceive the compelling motivation behind the writings of Hugh Black. His consistent objective is the transformation of lives by the grace and power of Christ. In his own words, 'The Holy Spirit faces men with a moral choice.' The absolute Lordship of Christ and the absolute discipleship demanded by Christ are pressed home on the serious reader as life-changing facts presented with clarity and without compromise.

The Messianic prophecies of the Old Testament are persuasively and convincingly shown to have their perfect fulfilment in Christ as revealed in the Gospels. Here Mr Black brings to bear his skill and experience as a professional teacher. A paraphrase of Jesus' own description of 'teachers' in Matthew 13:52 has an adaptable relevance here: 'Those teachers (of the law) who are now my disciples have double treasures—from the Old Testament as well as from the New.'

When Mr Black turns his attention to those 'final things' which concern our state after death and judgment he does not indulge in speculative Eschatology.

Academic brilliance may dismiss it, liberal theology may eliminate it and scientific thought may ridicule it, nevertheless 'Hell' remains a threat to every living soul. The cynical shrug or intellectual disdain are useless defences against the fearsome reality of 'Hell.' Few in our pulpits today have the courage and conviction necessary to proclaim the certainty of an eternal Hell. Few in our pews are willing to listen and discover that far from Hell being God's choice for any living soul it is in fact the consequence of our own choosing. For those willing to listen, Mr Black will leave the reader in no doubt as to the certainty of Hell and the absolute certainty of salvation from such a terrifying destiny, through Christ. What is even more astonishing is the degree of reluctance among church members to accept a clear unwavering belief in the reality of Heaven as promised by Christ.

When Christ promised to send us His Spirit 'to lead us into all truth,' He was offering us the key to that spiritual perception and conviction that leaves us in no doubt concerning the equal realities of Heaven and Hell. With painstaking attention to clarity and detail therefore, Mr Black takes the true seeker after God step by step to that essential experience of the birth of the Spirit in the life of a believer. Only the Holy Spirit can cure spiritual blindness and open our eyes to spiritual realities.

When he refers to Christ as 'the revolutionary,' Mr Black is not joining the array of political agitators advocating social revolution. Christ empties the word 'revolution' of its human origins and gives it new content. Christ's revolution concerns itself with the heart of man where He overthrows the ruling junta comprising 'the World,' 'the Flesh' and 'the Devil.' In their place He installs the control of the Holy Spirit. Mr Black expands for the reader the far-reaching implications for those who willingly respond to the rule of Christ 'the revolutionary.'

Mr Black's inclusion of personal testimonies in his recent books has added a fascinating dimension. Names become personalities and the endless variety of the workings of the Holy Spirit becomes visibly incarnate in ordinary lives to the Glory of Christ.

There is a refreshing openness and transparent honesty about the twins Susie and Pauline as their story unfolds. The Holy Spirit has obvious freedom to move in and through their lives, giving rise to a spontaneous thankfulness to God that they should be set apart to develop their caring ministry in helping others find release from bondage. Susie's specific descriptions of what the 'visual' gift can mean in the deliverance ministry is helpful in our understanding of the depth and power of evil which we are called to combat, overcome and where necessary exorcise.

Pauline's testimony, written whilst at the bedside of her dying mother, grips the heart and rivets the attention from the outset.

The exclamation 'Oh God!' can be no more than a cursory ejaculation but at other times it can express the inexpressible in prayer, as Pauline reveals. Born again of the Spirit and baptised with the Spirit she yearned desperately to be totally consecrated to God and it was when God answered this brief but sincere cry that her life became completely realigned to the service of Christ and ready to enter the spiritual combat in the power of Christ.

As well as their own special relationship as twins Susie and Pauline obviously enjoyed a close bond of affection with their parents. Despite initial misgivings their mother and father never unduly opposed their daughters' decision to leave the Roman Catholic Church and make a Pentecostal church their operational base for serving Christ. How wonderful that Susie and Pauline should have the joy of seeing their parents come to know Christ as their Saviour. What a benediction that they live daily in the certainty of being reunited in Heaven.

Truly God is no one's debtor!

Rev Alec Porteous

Preface

The first part of this book deals with themes that are amongst the most important that ever engage the minds of men. It concentrates on issues of life and death, of Time and Eternity. It presents Christ as He really is and faces the reader with the challenge of His life and personality and with the age-enduring and world-wide effect of His teachings. It calls for action. It points out the folly of any man gaining the world at the price of losing his own soul. It faces honestly the questions of Christ's resurrection and that of all men. It speaks of the power of the gospel and deals in a direct way with the doctrine of hell and eternal judgment, and finally it gives practical instruction on the Way of Salvation.

The second part of the book contains the story of two young ladies, twins, who have had their own individual encounters with Christ and have found that He has transformed their lives. Their experiences could encourage others.

PART 1

THE INCOMPARABLE CHRIST

Introduction

The title of this book was chosen before I realised that a piece of prose/poetry had already appeared with the same name. I was familiar with this writing and had indeed planned to include it in this book, but I knew it under the title 'The Unique Christ.' In the circumstances I have allowed the title of the book to stand.

The first part of the work has concentrated on three vital questions, two from the lips of Christ and one from Pilate: *What think ye of Christ? What shall I do with Jesus Who is called Christ?* and *What shall it profit a man if he gains the whole world and loses his own soul?* The answers to these questions are of life changing significance. A fourth chapter considers the question of truth. It too came from the lips of Pilate when Christ stood before him: *What is truth?*

Remembering the frame of mind of many enquirers and the problem they have with the resurrection I have included two chapters on this: 'Do the Dead Live?' and 'Indeed they Do!' The resurrection is a vital truth and rests on what I consider incontrovertible evidence. The case is far stronger than many imagine.

Remembering also the distorted view of Christ that is sometimes presented and knowing from long experience how youth reacts to this, I have tried to show Him as He really is—strong, vital, courageous, aiming to change a world—a revolutionary. Jesus Christ was no anaemic, weak, stained-glass window caricature.

This is followed by a fearful chapter—simply, 'Hell.' This is a doctrine so painful that many of us instinctively shy away from it and good men have often tried to blot it out altogether; but truth still stands and we must face the clear teaching of Christ—but we approach it softly with bowed heads. The truth itself is so terrible that it need not always be shouted from the housetops. Tenderness and compassion are needed in its presentation.

The last chapter is included to give practical help to those seeking to come to terms with Christ and His message. So many just do not know what to do, nor how to do what is essential in conversion. From painful personal experience in this area I try to make things clear and simple for others.

The Incomparable Christ is the first of two books on the gospel. The second, *Gospel Vignettes*, is expected to be published shortly.

1

What Do You *Think of Christ?*

It has been said that any fool can ask a question but it often takes a wise man to answer. When the Questioner turns out to be the Son of God we will do well to give His question serious consideration.

The five simple words, *What think ye of Christ?* (Mt 22:42) first burst upon the ears of people who were already speculating about the identity of Jesus. His works were mighty—indeed unparalleled—and some thought He might be Elijah returned, or John the Baptist risen from the dead. Others dismissed Him as merely a carpenter's son from Nazareth. Ever deep in the Jewish mind was the question of the coming Messiah. He had been promised from of old and expectation had grown through the ages and was perhaps never more alive than when the nation was either in captivity or occupied by a foreign power. But there were difficulties with the concept of the Messiah. Scripture seemed to contradict itself—which of course it never could. One line of prophecy quite clearly predicted a coming King of Whose Kingdom there would be no end:

> For unto us a child is born, unto us a son is given; and the government shall be upon his shoulder: and his name shall be

> called Wonderful, Counsellor, Mighty God, Everlasting Father, Prince of Peace. Of the increase of his government and of peace there shall be no end, upon the throne of David, and upon his kingdom, to establish it, and to uphold it with judgement and with righteousness from henceforth even for ever (Is 9:6–7).

Another line as emphatically spoke of a suffering Saviour who would die for His people:

> Surely he hath borne our griefs, and carried our sorrows.... But he was wounded for our transgressions, he was bruised for our iniquities: the chastisement of our peace was upon him; and with his stripes we are healed...he poured out his soul unto death... (Is 53:4–5, 12).

I can well imagine the attention which the learned rabbis would give to this question. They knew that the Messiah would be born in Bethlehem, and Scripture made it clear that He would be called out of Egypt. He would be a Man of Sorrows and acquainted with grief. He would sit on the throne of His father David and His Kingdom would be everlasting. No bone of Him would be broken, yet they would look on Him Whom they pierced. He would be despised and rejected of men but highly exalted of God. The problem seemed impossible to solve, and no doubt there were echoes of it in every Jewish mind. It is against this background that Christ appeared on the world's stage, and already His early life had fulfilled prophecy. He had, as predicted, been Virgin-born of David's line and had also been born in Bethlehem; He had gone into Egypt and been called back from Egypt. The voice of weeping and lamentation had been heard in Ramah and a voice had sounded from Heaven: 'This is My beloved Son in Whom I am well pleased.' But in no way was the fundamental problem of the two different lines of prophecy any nearer solution in that day. I can well imagine the sceptics and the critics then and indeed through the ages pointing jeeringly at the Scriptures and saying, 'The Messiah is going to die, is He? How then can He live for ever? He is a suffering Saviour and a ruling King: can't the writers make up their minds?'[1]

We who live in a later day have no such problem. Both lines of prophecy apply to the same Person—but to that Person at different points in time. In His first advent He was the suffering Saviour; in His second He will be the ruling King, and indeed much of His own teaching refers to His coming again.

Thus for His hearers Christ's question, 'What think ye of Christ?' was difficult but also highly relevant. And when we ponder the matter we realise it has been relevant to all succeeding ages. Christ cannot be ignored. He forever demands an answer. He divided men in His own day; He has divided them ever since. He divided time itself into BC and AD. He made the supreme claim of being the Son of God and the only way by which fallen man could get back to God. He promised to satisfy human need utterly and redeem the souls of men. 'Whosoever drinketh of the water that I shall give him shall never thirst' (Jn 4:14). He claimed unconditional loyalty from His every follower and intimated that those who did not become His followers would perish for ever. What a personality! What a claim!

> Now on the last day, the great day of the feast, Jesus stood and cried, saying, If any man thirst, let him come unto me, and drink. He that believeth on me, as the scripture hath said, out of his belly shall flow rivers of living water (Jn 7:37–38).

And again He said:

> Come unto me, all ye that labour and are heavy laden, and I will give you rest (Mt 11:28).
>
> Him that cometh to me I will in no wise cast out (Jn 6:37).

Of Heaven He said, 'I am the way' to it, but again, 'Except

that ye believe that I am he, ye shall die in your sins' (Jn 8:24); and of some he said, 'Whither I go, ye cannot come' (Jn 8:21). Surely, 'In the place where the tree falleth, there shall it be' (Ec 11:3).

When we stand back from the immediate life of Christ and see that life in its historical perspective we face a tremendous challenge. Another has written of Him as follows:

> *Here is a young man who was born in an obscure village, the child of a peasant woman. He grew up in another village. He worked in a carpenter's shop until he was 30, and then for three years he was an itinerant preacher. He never wrote a book. He never held office. He never owned a home. He never had a family. He never went to college. He never put his foot inside a big city. He never travelled 200 miles from the place where he was born. He never did one of the things that usually accompany greatness. He had no credentials but himself.*
>
> *While he was still a young man, the tide of public opinion turned against him. His friends ran away. One of them betrayed Him; another denied Him. He was turned over to his enemies. He went through the mockery of a trial. He was nailed to a cross between two thieves. While he was dying, his executioners gambled for the only piece of property he had on earth, and that was his coat. When he was dead, he was laid in a borrowed grave through the pity of a friend.*
>
> *Nineteen centuries have come and gone, and today he is the central figure of the human race and leader of the column of progress.*
>
> *I am far within the mark when I say that all the armies that ever marched, and all the navies that were ever built, and all the parliaments that ever sat, and all the kings that ever reigned, put together, have not affected the life of man upon this earth as powerfully as has that One Solitary Life.*[2]

A second unknown writer continues:

> *Almost twenty centuries ago there was a Man born contrary to the laws of life. His death was contrary to the laws of death. He*

lived in poverty and was reared in obscurity. He did not travel extensively. Only once did He cross the boundary of the country in which He lived; that was during His exile in childhood. He possessed neither wealth nor influence. His relatives were inconspicuous and had neither training nor formal education. He possessed neither wealth nor social prestige.

In infancy He startled a king; in childhood He puzzled doctors; in manhood He ruled the course of nature, walked upon the billows as pavements, and hushed the sea to sleep.

He had no cornfields or fisheries, but He could spread a table for five thousand and have bread and fish to spare.

He healed the multitudes without medicine and made no charge for His service.

He never wrote a book, and yet all the libraries of the country could not hold the books that have been written about Him.

He never wrote a song, and yet He has furnished the theme for more songs than all the songwriters combined.

He never founded a college, but all the schools put together cannot boast of having as many students.

He never marshalled an army, nor drafted a soldier, nor fired a gun; and yet no leader ever had more volunteers who have, under His orders, made more rebels stack arms and surrender without a shot fired.

He never practiced psychiatry, and yet He has healed more broken hearts than all the doctors far and near.

When He died few men mourned. But a black crepe was hung over the sun. Though men trembled not for their sins, the earth beneath them shook under the load. All nature honoured Him. Sinners alone rejected Him. Corruption could not get hold of His body. The soil that had been reddened with His blood could not claim His dust.

Once each week the wheels of commerce cease their turning and multitudes wend their way to worshipping assemblies to pay homage and respect to Him.

The names of past, proud statesmen of Greece and Rome have come and gone. The names of past scientists and philosophers have come and gone, but the name of this Man abounds more and more. Though time has spread nearly 2,000 years between the people of this generation and the scene of His crucifixion, yet

> *He still lives. Herod could not destroy Him, and the grave could not hold Him.*
>
> *He stands forth upon the highest pinnacle of heavenly glory, proclaimed of God, acknowledged by angels, adored by saints, and feared by devils, as the living, personal Christ, our Lord and Saviour.*
>
> *Was it merely the son of Joseph and Mary who crossed the world's horizon almost 2,000 years ago? Was it merely human blood that was spilled at Calvary's Hill for the redemption of sinners?*
>
> *Like Thomas, could anyone in their right mind keep from exclaiming:* "My Lord and my God!"[3]

Shall we look more closely at His life again?

He taught as one having authority and not as the scribes and Pharisees. He claimed to be the Son of God. He supported that claim by miraculous works. He healed the sick and raised the dead. He multiplied the loaves and fish miraculously and therewith fed multitudes. With a word He stilled the storm. He walked on water. His teaching was sublime and age enduring. Demons fled at His Presence and His command. His mighty miracles were witnessed by the crowds—but less noticeable at first may have been the age-enduring miracle of the change He worked, and goes on working, in the lives of those who became His followers. He broke their bonds and set them free. He forgave their sins and gave them new life. He radically transformed life. From selfishness and self-centredness men were delivered into God-centredness. Instead of being consumed with self-love they began to love God and their fellows. Their motivation changed. This is indeed remarkable and is produced by no religion other than Christianity. Yes, indeed, there has never been another like Christ. His life was unique. We view Him in His miraculous birth, His glorious ministry and shameful death, and from beginning to end find no flaw in Him—a perfect character, a perfect life and a perfect death. Well might we say with the writer of 'Ecce Homo':

> *Nineteen hundred years and more*
> *Upon Judean hills*
> *A character of wondrous blending*
> *Suddenly appeared,*
> *The Man of Destiny—man destined to be,*
> *In profile projected, by prophets predicted,*
> *By all ages desired, by archangels admired,*
> *Like man He walked. Like God He talked.*
> *His words were oracles. His acts were miracles.*
> *Of God the best expression,*
> *Of man the finest specimen,*
> *Full orbed humanity crowned with Divinity,*
> *No taint of iniquity, no trace of impurity:*
> Ecce homo—*Behold the man;*
> Ecce Deus—*Behold thy God.*

When we lift our eyes again to the wider canvas and consider Christ's influence on history we must needs stand back in amazement. He was born in an obscure corner of Galilee, in a village of poor repute at a time when His nation was under the yoke of Rome. He grew up in obscurity and after a few brief years of ministry He was taken by the Roman power, unjustly judged and crucified between two thieves. He was deserted by His few humble followers at His death. As we have been reminded, He had written no book, nor had He founded an institution of learning. He died in obscurity—yet today He is worshipped as God by untold millions, and has been through the ages. We must needs face the question as Napoleon did in a later day: 'Can this be the Christ?'

What has been His influence on the world? Who can fully tell it? In a peculiar way men have recognised it in accepting the fact that He alone of all humanity has divided time itself by His birth. He was born into a barbarous world—a world of cruelty and pain. But he so taught that His teachings have profoundly affected that world. He showed a way of love and righteousness and gradually His influence had its effect. Light began to affect the darkness. His ideas moved the hearts of men and nations. By their millions men became His followers. His influence affected the laws of the western world until a point has been reached where all men are affected in some measure by the life of Christ—either directly or indirectly. For example, there are many who do not feel for Him the slightest allegiance, yet they live in a land whose institutions, laws and customs have been profoundly influenced by His teachings. I am reminded of the story of an incident which took place at Hyde Park when a Christian preacher was being interrupted by an atheist. The latter was demanding to know what Christianity had ever done for the world. I do not remember all the details accurately but the gist of the story was that a mature Christian rose and took the platform. Pointing north, south, east and west, he indicated hospitals and charitable institutions all over London which had been founded by Christians. His opponent slunk away.[4] What we owe Christ in terms of decency and justice apart altogether from eternal life is far beyond our ability to assess.

I come back to Napoleon. There in exile on St. Helena, a broken and defeated man, he was considering his life. He realised that his bid for glory was over and as he recalled his fallen empire he began to think of Christ and compare his empire with Christ's. His had been founded on force and military might; Christ's on love. He had ascended his throne over the broken bodies of men; Christ had given His own body to be broken for the life of the world. He had sailed through seas of blood to his desired haven; Christ had shed His own blood for His people. There in bitter exile Napoleon is said to have exclaimed as he pondered the two empires, 'Tonight there is not a sword in Europe that would be unsheathed for me, yet millions would gladly die for Him. Can this be the Christ?' To which we can but reply: Who else? Who else?

There are two further quotations which I would like to bring to you before asking again the question: 'What think ye of Christ?'

Most Bible students have at least a vague notion that there was a good deal of prophecy in the Old Testament about the coming Messiah—but few perchance have systematically studied the subject. It may come as a surprise to read the conclusions of two scholars who did so. They are profoundly moving.

Herbert Lockyer has written:

> The literal fulfillment of a prophecy is the seal of its divine origin. Prophecies of centuries concerning the final sufferings of Christ were fulfilled during the twenty-four hours leading up to His crucifixion. According to the law of compound probabilities, the chance that they all happened together by accident is 1 in 537,000,000.
>
> In Pierson's *God's Living Oracles*, this renowned Bible scholar says that there are
>
>> Over 300 predictions about the Messiah to be found in the Old Testament. According to the law of compound probability, the chance of their coming true is represented by a fraction whose numerator is one, and the denominator eighty-four followed by nearly one hundred ciphers. One might almost as well expect by accident to dip up any one particular drop out of the ocean as to expect so many prophetic rays to converge by chance upon one man, in one place, at one time. God has put especially upon these prophecies as to His Son the *stamp of absolute* verity and indisputable certainty, so that we may know whom we have believed. Mistakes in so solemn a matter are fatal and God meant that none should be possible.[5]

Josh McDowell takes up the same theme: from over three hundred Old Testament prophecies regarding Christ he particularly identifies sixty-one and shows their fulfilment. In dealing with the critic's objection that fulfilled prophecy in Jesus might be coincidental, or accidental, and that one might say: 'Why, you could find some of these prophecies fulfilled in Kennedy, King, Nasser, etc.,' he wrote:

> Yes, one could possibly find one or two prophecies fulfilled in other men, but not all 61 major prophecies!...
>
> The following probabilities are taken from Peter Stoner in *Science Speaks* to show that coincidence is ruled out by the science of probability. Stoner says that by using the modern science of probability in reference to eight prophecies... "We find that the chance that any man might have lived down to the present time and fulfilled all eight prophecies is 1 in 10^{17}." That would be 1 in 100,000,000,000,000,000. In order to help us comprehend this staggering probability, Stoner illustrates it by supposing that "we take 10^{17} silver dollars and lay them on the face of Texas. They will cover all of the state two feet deep. Now mark one of these silver dollars and stir the whole mass thoroughly, all over the state. Blindfold a man and tell him that he can travel as far as he wishes, but he must pick up one silver dollar and say that this is the right one. What chance would he have of getting the right one? Just the same chance that the prophets would have had of writing these eight prophecies and having them all come true in any one man, from their day to the present time, providing they wrote them in their own wisdom.
>
> 'Now these prophecies were either given by inspiration of God or the prophets just wrote them as they thought they should be. In such a case the prophets had just one chance in 10^{17} of being absolute.
>
> Stoner considers 48 prophecies and says, "...We find the chance that any one man fulfilled all 48 prophecies to be 1 in 10^{157}.[6]

Yes, indeed we are overwhelmed with evidence and must say with the Roman soldier as he stood at the cross, 'Truly this was the Son of God.' May I ask *you* again: *What think ye of Christ?*

Notes

[1] It would be wrong to suppose that all Jews realised the problem that Scripture posed on this question. No doubt honest enquirers searched diligently to know what the Spirit indicated, but the prevalent, and I might say the official, view held by the religious leaders was of a glorious Messiah, and awkward writings which presented the other side of this truth tended to be given distorted interpretations. Thus when Christ came He did not fit into the current Messianic dream and indeed had to fight against it with words like: 'My kingdom is not of this world.' The commonly held view was a barrier to His work. His teaching was not the teaching expected of the Messiah. The way of humility and love found no answer in hearts hungry for national power and greatness. Even His miracles were generally performed for the good of individuals and were not of the spectacular type expected of the Messiah. An evil and adulterous generation sought after signs for signs' sake. Christ did not supply that kind. He did not stop the sun in its course to demonstrate His power. He stilled the waves in a very private situation to save His disciples. To the power-hungry, materially-minded Israelites He was a great disappointment. Even many of His *followers* were offended in Him and many who once followed left Him. Instead of world-shaking works of power to astonish the nation, such as throwing Himself down from the top of the temple so that all might believe on Him, He went in and out quietly amongst men 'doing good and healing all who were oppressed of the devil.' For further illumination on this question, see Otto Borchert, *The Original Jesus*, trans. from the German by L. M. Stalker (Lutterworth Press, 1933). On the two Messiahs in Jewish theology, see Appendix One.

[2] 'One Solitary Life' (author unknown). This extract appears with minute variations; I have slightly modified the present version.

[3] 'The Incomparable Christ,' also published as 'The Unique Christ' (author unknown to me). My rendering of this extract, which varies more widely than the preceding, is based mainly on the version quoted in Josh McDowell, *Evidence that Demands a Verdict: Historical Evidences for the Christian Faith* (rev. ed., Here's Life Publishers, Inc., 1979), p. 135.

[4] This interrupter got off rather more lightly than a communist heckler of whom the late Professor Joad tells us. He was rather a dirty and unkempt individual, and he had been troubling a preacher at the same venue on another occasion, complaining that there had been Christianity in the world for almost two thousand years—'and look,' he said, 'at the state of the world.' Quick as an arrow came back the reply: 'There has been soap and water in the world for more than two thousand years, and look at the state of your neck!' All the man had to do was apply it. So with Christianity: it must not be dismissed as ineffective before it is practised.

[5] Herbert Lockyer, *All the Messianic Prophecies of the Bible* (Zondervan, 1973), p. 17.

[6] McDowell, *Evidence that Demands a Verdict*, pp. 166–67. For readers particularly interested in this type of study, I include further material from McDowell's work in Appendix Two.

2

What is Truth?

Our second question arises as an insertion before we consider the third, which is, *What shall I do with Jesus which is called Christ?* The third has a natural connection with the first: *What think ye of Christ?* Having considered His Person and His claims there comes an almost inevitable challenge—what will we do with Him? As I indicated earlier, He cannot be ignored. He demands an answer. One Whose life and teachings were so significant, that almost 2,000 years later every major university in the western world has faculties whose main studies focus around His teaching, must be treated with all seriousness. If we study the circumstances in which the question was first asked by Pilate, we will learn that it was almost immediately preceded by another question: *What is truth?* (Jn 18:38) And again and again men must face the same question before they decide on a final response to Christ.

It is not my intention in this book to go into detail about the philosophical overtones in such a question. The problem of truth, or epistemology, to give it its technical connotation, has through the ages been uppermost in the minds of the western world's deepest thinkers, and many and varied have been the answers given. Our present enquiry need involve no vague or abstract philosophising. It is straightforward and spiritually simple.

Imagine again the circumstances in which the question was first asked: Christ had been arraigned before Pilate on false charges and His enemies sought His death. Pilate was in a weak position and those enemies were strong. There had been repeated trouble between the Roman governor and the subjugated nation—so much so that a further insurrection might be very seriously viewed by Caesar. Pilate might well have suspected that his career was suspended on a very slender thread and that he could not afford to alienate further the Jews whose hatred he had already incurred. And so the hour came when Christ's enemies were baying for His blood. Pilate, not known as a scrupulous judge, was far from satisfied with any real evidence on which he could base a conviction and he enquired as to what evil Christ had done. To this came the answer that He made Himself a king and that He was seditious. Pilate soon elicited from Christ the fact that He had laid claim to no earthly kingdom—else His servants would have fought. He went on to say, 'To this end have I been born, and to this end am I come into the world, that I should bear witness unto the truth. Everyone that is of the truth heareth my voice' (Jn 18:37). To which Pilate replied, 'What is truth?'

We may never know how seriously or how lightly Pilate asked the question, but he does not appear to have waited for a reply or further enlightenment.

I want you now to view two scenes—one on the surface of life as seen by the world in general: a second hidden beneath the outward appearance of events.

Christ stood there falsely accused, and neither Herod nor Pilate found any guilt in Him. Indeed Pilate was compelled to the confession: 'I have found no cause of death in Him' (Lk 23:22), and he desired to release him. But the pressures were too strong for him. The Jews determinedly called not merely for punishment and torture but for the death sentence—which they could not themselves impose. Despite his tormented wife's pleas, Pilate called for a basin in which he ceremonially washed his hands, indicating that he was not being responsible for the blood of Christ. Gladly the Jews assumed the responsibility and showed no fear of that blood coming on them and on their children. Pilate may have thought he washed his hands in water and in innocency. We judge that he washed them in blood and murder. So with calls for the releasing of Barabbas the murderer ringing in his ears Pilate made the fearful decision. The young Teacher who had so troubled the hypocritical Pharisees and materialistic Saducees was delivered to further torture, lashing and crucifixion. Pilate with a seared conscience went home. The blood-lusting crowd prevailed and dire injustice was perpetrated.

Such was the surface scene and so might it have been recorded by any unbiased onlooker. There might, no doubt, have been questions left unanswered. Why, for example, was there such rage and hatred against one so kindly and so obviously sincere? Why were the multitude so determined to have Him crucified when they had sung their loud hosannas so shortly before—when He came riding in triumph into Jerusalem? Why did such a miracle worker as Christ perform no miracle on His own behalf? Why did He so meekly endure the cross and show no resentment, praying, 'Father, forgive them, for they know not what they do?'—and why did the earth shake and why was the sky darkened for three hours as He finally expired on the cross? And finally, if He was the promised Messiah, the Son of God, why did God allow the whole sequence and culmination of events? Who could believe that the God of all the universe would allow creatures of the dust so to treat His Beloved Son? We who live after the event and who know and love the Christ may answer, at least in some measure, all of the questions posed. To a man of Christ's own day, they must, however, have been very real and very difficult.

There is a second scene—an inner scene. On the surface Christ stands at the tribunal of man to be judged of him. In reality Pilate stands as a representative of man at the tribunal of God to be judged of Him. Christ is being weighed in the scales of human justice: Pilate, though he knew it not, found himself on the balances of God. On the surface Pilate may have given an impression of dignity and power: beneath the surface he was a troubled soul—with an outraged sense of being driven to perpetrate injustice, with concern for his dream-troubled wife and no doubt for his own position if not his own safety. To a conscience about to be irrevocably seared by a cowardly decision he did not wish to make, came the words of Christ in answer to his question 'What is truth?': 'If any man willeth to do [God's] will, he shall know of the teaching, whether it be of God, or whether I speak from myself' (Jn 7:17). Christ here looks right into the soul of man and virtually says: 'Any man who wants to know the truth about Me can know it. Pilate, if you are a true man, you will recognise truth. My teaching is the truth of God and My will is the will of God. If any man is willing to do My will, he will know the truth.' Many a man professes to wish to know the truth about Christ and maintains that if he only knew he would obey. God says, 'My friend, you can know if you really want to know.' Sometimes the knowing seems easier than the obeying and the truth seems too costly. So Pilate wanted to know what truth was: little did he realise that he would face truth, and highly unpalatable truth, in a very few moments after asking his question. The truth for him involved moral decision. He knew that Christ was an innocent man and no stirrer of sedition. He knew that no credible evidence had been laid against Him. He knew that for envy and jealousy the Jews had delivered Him up.

He knew all these things. There was no doubt about the truth—but he also knew how precarious his own position was. He knew the rage and malice of the Jews, not only against Christ but potentially against himself. When it came to judgment he knew the truth. He knew what he ought to do—but he had neither the courage nor the character to do it.

After attempting to evade an inconvenient decision by releasing Jesus, as he could legitimately do by customary right without giving judgment, he was faced with the Jews' choice of Barabbas instead of Christ. Pilate then realised that he could no longer avoid a choice. This was the critical moment. This was the point where the moral decision was made. Pilate was lost at this point—as are countless others through the ages, though circumstances differ. Before he made his choice regarding what to do with Christ, he had to settle a moral question—a question of right and wrong: he knew what he ought to do and what he ought to do not only for Christ but for any man who appeared in his court. He made a wrong moral decision and all the later sequence of events flowed from it. He betrayed the law of human justice and gave a false judgment.

Again and again enquirers express interest in Christ and salvation, and on examination prove to be seriously in breach of moral law and to have no sincere intention of proper living. Again and again the Holy Spirit faces men with a moral choice, and until it is made they are granted no entry to the Kingdom. The door does not open. The light does not dawn. Finney very strongly emphasised this principle. I seem to remember that a man once came to him with intellectual difficulties about salvation, professing not to know what to do. Finney asked him if he was fully obeying the measure of light he already had. The answer to this was in the negative and Finney refused to deal with the case until the man put the matter right. This he did and with it his problems disappeared and he found Christ without further help.

To illustrate this principle in an earlier work, I referred to an occasion when a young soldier, about to be demobilised at the end of the last war, expressed an interest in salvation at an open-air meeting. On being counselled he indicated that he wanted to postpone decision until after a certain date because of a party which his friends were holding and which he wished to attend. He knew there would be ongoings there which would be inconsistent with Christian conduct and he did not wish to be unable to take part in them. He postponed commitment to Christ and arranged to see me on a later date. We made the arrangement but he failed to turn up. I never saw him, nor expected to see him, again. You daren't work this way with God. Real, thorough and complete repentance is necessary—a right attitude is always essential. Pilate was weighed in the balances and was found wanting.

From his fatal fall at this hurdle he was rushed on by events beyond his control to the point where he shouted the awful question to his tormentors, who would not be satisfied except with the release of Barabbas the thieving murderer. Release was for either Barabbas or Christ. The Jewish rulers and the mob were determined that it would be Barabbas. Not the Christ, the sinless Son of God. 'What then,' said Pilate, 'shall I do with Jesus who is called Christ?' (Mt 27:22).

3

What will You *Do with Christ?*

And so our next chapter opens with the agonising question from the lips of Pilate: *What then shall I do with Jesus Who is called Christ?'* There is a sense in which we see Pilate here in the role of Everyman, although our circumstances are all different. The whole wide world faces the question.

In Pilate's case a wrong moral decision betrayed him in this crisis hour. Fear of the Jews, fear of Caesar, fear for himself were all too much for him and he plunged to moral death as he delivered Christ over to be crucified. See the picture—see behind the outward scenes. Christ stood to be judged of Pilate. He was condemned and went out one door to scourging and torment, by the Via Dolorosa to Calvary's hill, by way of the Cross and an agonising death to victory and eternal glory—a conqueror for ever. I often wish I had the gift of the artist. I would love to paint the face of Christ as He sank beneath the dark waters of the river of death. See Him going down with head held high, never defeated; and on that glorious face, albeit wracked with pain, would shine the light of the glory of God. He was not holden of death but rose victoriously to everlasting life and joy. He died and rose again a conqueror.

Pilate on the other hand sat on his judgment throne and pronounced the words that condemned himself for ever. He rose and went through another door to a turbulent future. The Jews whom he feared and tried to placate proved revengeful. The Caesar whom he feared to offend was still offended and, if secular history is correct, sent Pilate to banishment in southern Italy, where he died a suicide's death. And what of the life beyond? I cannot but fear that Pilate went out of this life a lost soul—bound for an eternal hell.

It could have been so different—oh, the might-have-beens of life. If only he had bitten the bullet, had stood as Luther stood in a later day and said before God and men, 'Here I stand. I can do no other. May God help me. I find no fault in Christ. I refuse to condemn Him. Release Him and let Him go.' 'But, Pilate, you may lose your life.' 'Yes, indeed I may, but I would rather lose my life than my soul. I would rather die with a good conscience than go on living with one that is seared.' May I suggest that had he done it his name would have lived for ever. He would have been regarded as a hero by all after ages, and his portion in the world to come would almost certainly have been eternal life. I feel certain that had he crossed the moral bridge he would have known the power of the word: 'He shall know of the teaching,' and again, 'Ye shall know the truth and the truth shall make you free.'

It was not to be. The whole world knows that the Christ suffered under Pontius Pilate, and Pilate's name is for ever associated with ignominy and shame. Sometimes he is pitied as a poor weakling. And it is easy to judge Pilate and many another who has sold the Christ for a handful of silver, or a career, or friends or social position—but what of ourselves? We too must meet the same question: What will I do with Jesus Who is called the Christ?

The words of the hymn come hauntingly to mind:

Jesus is standing in Pilate's hall—
  Friendless, forsaken, betrayed by all:
Hearken! what meaneth the sudden call?
  What will you do with Jesus?

What will you do with Jesus?
  Neutral you cannot be;
Some day your heart will be asking,
  "What will He do with me?"

Our position is very different from that of the Jews. Their background was such that it was generally enough for any one of them, on recognising Jesus as the Messiah, to become from that moment His devoted follower. To ignore Him would have been unthinkable. To acknowledge His claim to full allegiance and authority followed automatically from the recognition of His identity.

Matters are far different with us. With no fervent tradition of a coming Messiah in the background, we hear of Christ and read of His miraculous life and death. We ponder His teachings and make our intellectual assessments. Even when we come to the point of recognising that His was a unique life we have no necessary conviction that we should become His servants. Even when we come to the point of conviction that He is the Son of God and that He has atoned for our sins and we accept His offer of salvation—may I say it to our shame that too frequently we are still largely ignorant of our obligation to come fully under His Lordship.

For many a long day I found great difficulty in understanding what the vital ingredients of salvation really were. On enquiring, as a boy, I was told I had to believe on Christ. I didn't quite understand what this meant and questioned more closely precisely what I should believe—what was the vital part? I was told that to believe really meant to believe that He had died for my sins on Calvary and that my believing this was sufficient. I read the Bible carefully and realised that it did teach that He had died for my sins on the cross—but nowhere did I read that believing this fact would give me salvation. I studied deeply and discovered that when belief on Christ was enjoined the reference was always to His Messiahship and it ultimately dawned on me that for a Jew to recognise this meant subjection to His Lordship. The latter was inevitably involved.

We must consider this carefully. Too often there is a vagueness about the area of discipleship amongst professed Christians. What is the position and what does God expect? In my opinion there is not the distinction between salvation and consecration that some teachers might suggest. Because salvation is so frequently misunderstood and so inadequately presented, enquirers are given a hope and told, perhaps on little more than the expression of a willingness to be saved, that the wondrous gift is theirs. Questions of total and unconditional surrender to the will of God are not raised. Repentance or conviction of sin may be lightly passed over. Sincere people may find that their first introduction to Christ is of this type, and very soon they realise as they read their Bibles that God makes very deep demands on lives. For many in such positions the doctrine of full consecration becomes vital.

But things ought not to be so. When Christ encountered men He looked for full commitment and obedience. To Peter and Andrew the word was 'Follow Me.' To the rich young ruler He gave a command that demanded a depth of obedience that the man felt he could not give and he departed sorrowfully rather than renounce all that he had and follow Christ. To put it briefly: Christ makes an absolute demand on the life of His every follower. In another book I use an illustration which I feel will bear repeating here. During the American Civil War there came a point where the tide of battle turned against the

South, and they sent emissaries to meet Lincoln on a ship off the coast of America. Pointing to a map on the wall, they indicated their willingness to yield a boundary here and a town there, until Lincoln brought his hand down with a bang on the table with the words: 'This government, the government I represent, demands all.' There was to be unconditional surrender. There was to be no divided America. Now the Government I represent, the Government of Christ, demands all: there is to be unconditional surrender—no divided loyalty or allegiance.

This is the teaching of the New Testament. Salvation is not the consequence of a vague intellectual acceptance of a few truths about Jesus. It involves encounter with His Person by the operation of the Holy Spirit and a total submission to Him and an acceptance of Him not only as Saviour but as Lord. The taking of Him as Lord is a vital part of the contract into which the soul enters with God. Satan forever tries to prevent this happening and too often counsellors in their anxiety to count converts can be careless in dealing with enquirers. Again I would recommend the instruction of Finney on this matter. Search, he said, and find if there is a particular area on which the Holy Spirit is pressing the soul and make sure there is no evasion of the issue. When the sinner capitulates on this point he will almost certainly find salvation.

Now we must bring this truth, which was self-evident to the Jews of Christ's day, sharply to the minds of people with different backgrounds and traditions. We will find that all sorts of things are entertained in people's minds as being legitimate and essentially their own business. We will find that they view Christ as being 'over there,' as it were: the Son of God, yes; the Saviour of the World, yes; even their own Saviour—but not necessarily One to Whom absolute obedience in everything is essential. There can be a vast gulf between believing that Christ is the Son of God and even one's own Saviour, on one hand, and acknowledging and bowing to His Lordship, on the other.

So when such truth is clearly presented, what happens? The old nature fights to retain its own. Before the point of conversion there may be fear that He will interfere with a fond ambition, a wrong career. The soul may be in a wrong personal relationship with another and instinctively know that Christ will not allow it. There may be a lust for money, or power, or position. So many things present themselves, and there is an inner knowledge that we may have this or that or the other, but not along with Christ—and we have to choose. We do not all sell Him as Judas did for silver, or as Pilate through fear, or as the rich young ruler for wealth. Sometimes we sell Him for less. Quite simply we say by action: 'We will not have this man to rule over us.' What we do with the issues on which He seeks our obedience and allegiance so often determines what we do with Him. We make our choices as Pilate did. Shall we answer the question Pilate asked, 'What shall I do with Jesus Who is called Christ?' If we fail at the point on which the Spirit is pressing, we will fail as Pilate did on the issue of truth and there will be nothing left for us too than ultimately to reject and be rejected by Christ, as happened in Pilate's case.

In closing this chapter there come to mind the lines:

Is it nothing to you, all ye that pass by—
Is it nothing to you that Jesus should die?

I would recommend to my readers that they ponder deeply the significance of that death—its great cost and its relevance to the lives of all men. Perhaps one of the greatest sins of our age is not the deliberate rejection of Christ so much as our ignoring of Him. 'All right, He may have been the Son of God—but so what? All you say may be true, but I still want to live my own life my own way and get from it as much enjoyment as I possibly can. I don't want to be bothered with religion; I'm just not interested.'

May I put it pointedly to Everyman. If Jesus Christ was God and died for us, we may not ignore Him with impunity. God will one day call for an accounting as to what we did with His Son.

What then shall I do with Jesus Who is called Christ?

4

Is It Worth Losing Your Soul to Gain the World?

For what doth it profit a man, to gain the whole world, and forfeit his soul? (Mk 8:36)

Pilate found decision for Christ costly, so costly that he made the wrong choice, and countless others in Christ's own day and throughout the ages have faced what is really the same fundamental and life-changing decision. Christ Himself was deeply aware of the issues involved both in acceptance and in rejection of Him. It was no light peripheral or transient matter. It was for life or death—for time and eternity. Against this background His words fell with solemn impact: 'What doth it profit a man, to gain the whole world, and forfeit his life? For what should a man give in exchange for his soul?' It is as though He says: 'Consider this, weigh up the matter. Don't be foolish. Even if you gain the whole world by a wrong choice how good is your bargain if at the end you lose your own soul; that is, if you, yourself, are lost?' If we really consider this for a moment the irrefutable logic brings us up short.

Shall we consider the question and answer it from the lives of others. In addition to Pilate three characters spring to mind: Judas, Voltaire and Byron. Now obviously no man can possess the whole world nor did Christ suppose that he could—but it is equally true that a soul can covet a particular thing which becomes in him a dominant drive or obsession; and Christ says, 'Supposing you get that, as much as you can hold—your heart's deepest desire, even as much of it as you can possibly desire or possess—and at the end of the day are yourself lost as a result, what will your profit be?'

Judas was obsessed with money. He was a thief and had been stealing from the common purse. Christ obviously knew this but did not remove him from his position of treasurer for the company. He gave him every opportunity to repent and change his ways. Almost certainly Judas was attracted to Christ as a potential human potentate. He would have loved to rule with Him in an earthly kingdom. Christ exercised miraculous powers. It was very possible that he could lead the nation and break the yoke of Rome. I imagine that many a day-dream Judas enjoyed. As miracle followed miracle the goal would seem ever nearer. The sick were healed. The demon possessed set free. Even the dead were raised. The sea was calmed at a word. The multitudes were miraculously fed by the supernatural multiplication of loaves and fishes. Moreover again and again the people showed their willingness to follow Christ and as late as His last entrance to Jerusalem they sang their hosannas. Right up to this point Judas may well have retained hope; but there must have come a moment when this was totally dashed—when he finally realised that Christ really meant what He later put in clear words: 'My kingdom is not of this world.' Now the spiritual kingdom of which He spoke was of no interest to Judas: there were no high positions of state there; there was no money or material possession to be had there; rather there was a way of lowliness and humility, a way of poverty and sacrifice—a way that was totally unacceptable.

'Judas, you have journeyed with Him, observed His lifestyle, been close to Him through the years. Was He ever unkind, inconsiderate, selfish? How could you do other than love Him?'

'There were times I was enraged. He could so easily have got money out of the people. They would have followed Him—at one time they wanted to make Him a king but He refused. I held my dream, hoping until the end. I didn't think it possible that He would finally reject the way that would lead to the crown—but He did. Oh yes, while others loved, I hated. He frustrated me intolerably. One day he let a woman break an alabaster box and pour its costly ointment over Him. He had no thought of waste. Why, I could have sold that box for a fortune.'

So Judas retained his obsession and he retained it too long. We read the fearful words, 'then entered Satan into him.' Satan found a prepared channel. Men can so live that they become easy victims for the entrance of evil entities. Judas was one such. At the Last Supper Christ indicated that one of them would betray Him and they all wanted to know who it would be. Christ indicated to John that the one for whom He dipped the sop would be the traitor. Judas was identified and Christ raised His eyes and said, 'That thou doest, do quickly.' And Judas went out into the night. As one has said: He went out into the darkness, instigated by the prince of darkness to do a dark deed.

'You have made your choice, Judas. You have realised that there will be no earthly kingdom. You have tried to cut your losses and get at least some material gain out of Christ. You can betray Him to His enemies for at least some silver pieces.'

See the sorry scene. He gets his paltry pieces of silver and leads the soldiers to dark Gethsemane. He identifies Christ for them in the dim light. He does it with a kiss—supreme horror! And Christ, knowing of his perfidy, said:

'Betrayest thou the Son of man with a kiss?' The next part of the drama is, so far as it related to Judas, not played on the open stage. We next meet a demented man throwing his ill-gotten gain on the temple floor and it is left to our imagination to fill in the time between. The final scenes have been powerfully pictured by the late Dean Farrar in his *Life of Christ*. He wrote:

> Terribly soon did the Nemesis fall on the main actor in the lower stages of this iniquity. Doubtless through all those hours Judas had been a secure spectator of all that had occurred, and when the morning dawned upon that chilly night, and he knew the decision of the Priests and of the Sanhedrin, and saw that Jesus was now given over for crucifixion to the Roman Governor, then he began fully to realise all that he had done. There is in a great crime an awfully illuminating power. It lights up the theatre of the conscience with an unnatural glare, and, expelling the twilight glamour of self-interest, shows the actions and motives in their full and true aspect. In Judas, as in so many thousands before and since, this opening of the eyes which follows the consummation of an awful sin to which many other sins have led, drove him from remorse to despair, from despair to madness, from madness to suicide. Had he, even then, but gone to his Lord and Saviour, and prostrated himself at His feet to implore forgiveness, all might have been well. But, alas! he went instead to the patrons and associates and tempters of his crime. From them he met with no pity, no counsel. He was a despised and broken instrument, and now he was tossed aside. They met his maddening remorse with chilly indifference and callous contempt. "I have sinned," he shrieked to them, "in that I have betrayed innocent blood." Did he expect them to console his remorseful agony, to share the blame of his guilt, to excuse and console him with their lofty dignity! "What is that to us? See thou to that," was the sole and heartless reply they deigned to the poor traitor whom they had encouraged, welcomed, incited to his deed of infamy. He felt that he was of no importance any longer; that in guilt there is no possibility for mutual respect, no basis for any

> feeling but mutual abhorrence. His paltry thirty pieces of silver were all that he would get. For these he had sold his soul; and these he should no more enjoy than Achan enjoyed the gold he buried, or Ahab the garden he had seized. Flinging them wildly down upon the pavement into the holy place where the priests sat, and into which he might not enter, he hurried into the despairing solitude from which he would never emerge alive. In that solitude, we may never know what "unclean wings" were flapping about his head. Accounts differed as to the wretch's death. The probability is that the details were never accurately made public. According to one account, he hung himself, and tradition still points in Jerusalem to a ragged, ghastly, wind-swept tree, which is called the "tree of Judas." According to another version—not irreconcilable with the first, if we suppose that a rope or a branch broke under his weight—he fell headlong, burst asunder in the midst, and all his bowels gushed out (Acts 1:18).... The arch-conspirators, in their sanctimonious scrupulosity, would not put the blood-money which he had returned into the "Corban," or sacred treasury, but, after taking counsel, bought with it the potter's field to bury strangers in—a plot of ground which perhaps Judas had intended to purchase, and in which he met his end. That field was long known and shuddered at as the Aceldama, or "field of blood," a place foul, haunted, and horrible.[1]

So, Judas, you made your choice. For short-term gain you sold your Lord. What did it profit you? The words come thundering back. 'I have betrayed innocent blood—I am in an intolerable agony,' and casting the money on the temple floor he rushed out to his fearful death.

You may riposte, 'You have not proven your case; this man did not gain the world or anything like it in exchange for his soul; he gained but a pitiful pittance. Your illustration of Christ's words is unconvincing. Before replying let me quote from Farrar again:

> The narratives of the Synoptists point distinctly to avarice as the cause of his ruin.... How little insight can *they* have into

> the fatal bondage and diffusiveness of a besetting sin, into the dense spiritual blindness and awful infatuation with which it confounds the guilty, who cannot believe in so apparently inadequate a motive! Yet the commonest observance of daily facts which come before our notice in the moral world, might serve to show that the commission of crime results as frequently from a motive that seems miserably small and inadequate, as from some vast and abnormal temptation.... The sudden crisis of temptation might seem frightful, but its issue was decided by the entire tenor of his previous life; the sudden blaze of lurid light was but the outcome of that which had long burnt and smouldered deep within his heart.[2]

The world Judas sought to gain at the last was money. It had become his god—his goal—to many of us totally incomprehensible—but real enough to drive him on to destruction. We read that 'the whole world lieth in the wicked one,' and when Satan offered Christ the kingdoms of the world and the glory of them in the wilderness it was a real offer. He offered Christ the very thing He had come into the world to secure for His Father, but the offer involved a wrong means of securing a right end—a way that bypassed the Cross. Again and again Satan comes to men with the offer of the world, or as much of it as the soul desires—on evil terms which involve the loss of the soul. We may often wonder at what tempts others—at how little they value their souls. Some put social position, pleasure, career or a thousand and one other things before Christ—and when analysed, again and again the thing chosen is paltry: even when at first it may seem major, on close analysis it becomes minor. Nothing is worth the loss of the soul. Yet we seldom wonder at our own temptations.

Yes, Judas made a fearful bargain. Like Esau he sold not only his birthright but his very soul for a veritable mess of pottage. Let us ponder afresh the words of Christ:

> For what doth it profit a man, to gain the whole world, and forfeit his soul? For what should a man give in exchange for his soul? For whosoever shall be ashamed of me and of my words in this adulterous and sinful generation, the Son of man also shall be ashamed of him, when he cometh in the glory of his Father with the holy angels (Mk 8:36–38).

We pass on to Voltaire, the famous French infidel. If in the case of Judas he signally failed to gain the world, there is a sense in which Voltaire achieved this. Much of the eighteenth century worshipped at his feet. He played a vital role as one of the philosophers who had a powerful influence on the French Revolution, with its effect on the world. His was a brilliant mind and he received great adulation in his lifetime—but he was an infidel, and he was an infidel in an age and in a society in which he could have found God. The knowledge of God and the gospel was in the western world. I do not have a close knowledge of Voltaire's life and I do not know whether there was a time of particular crisis which affected his development, but I have chosen this life to illustrate one point. Here was a man who received the world's adulation—who could be said to have 'gained the world' in a very real sense, to have made a name that has lived through the centuries. 'What, Voltaire, has it profited you?' We attend the deathbed where he is reputed to have been questioned about his views and his condition. The words have been attributed to him: 'I wish I had never been born.' What words! What an epitaph! What a bad bargain this man must have made. In the face of the last great enemy death, all the world's adulation seems like a sick joke—an empty futile thing. Yes, Lord Jesus Christ, Your words fall as a melancholy knell upon this life: 'For what doth it profit a man, to gain the whole world, and forfeit his soul? For what should a man give in exchange for his soul?'

Let Byron come on to the stage—that proud, sinful dandy. Holding high social position in eighteenth century England he lived a life of debauchery and shame. Such was his behaviour that for long he had to live abroad. Not only did he live shamelessly but he gloried in his sin and yet strangely he was another who 'gained the world.' He was a brilliant poet and has always been recognised as such, in his own lifetime and down to our own day. Indeed on the Continent he has long been regarded as one of the three greatest English poets, although he is not accorded quite that position in Britain. Suffice that in this sphere he gained the world, and while much of his conduct scandalised many, he was still lionised and received his adulation in the literary world. Can we again go to the deathbed—very revealing places are deathbeds and, as one has said, 'Truth sits upon the lips of dying men.' How, Lord Byron, does life seem to you now? Gone are the women and the lechery, gone the drunkenness and debauchery. What remains? Have you made a good bargain? What, as you face the grim reaper whom we all must meet, have you to say of your state? Let us repeat them softly as the words have come down the years: 'The worm, the canker and the grief are mine alone.'

What did it profit these three men, Judas, Voltaire and Byron to have gained the world, or that part of it which they sought, and lost their souls? The words come ringing back:

I have betrayed innocent blood.
I wish I had never been born.
The worm, the canker and the grief are mine alone.

And I believe that, if we could draw back the curtain that separates the living from the dead, we would hear these same cries ringing to all eternity. Christ drew back the curtain one day and showed us the rich man in hell and indicated that he was in an agony, that he remembered his earth life and that between him and the abode of the blest there was an impassable gulf. No sophistry or wishful thinking has ever altered these facts. But oh, you say, Christ was speaking figuratively here. He was giving a parable. Was He? Then what, my friend, think you was the fearful reality which He was depicting? It is inescapable. *For what doth it profit a man, to gain the whole world, and forfeit his soul? For what should a man give in exchange for his soul?* The gain of these three men was utter loss. Let us learn the lesson.

Notes

[1] F. W. Farrar, *The Life of Christ* (pop. ed., Cassell, Petter, Galbin & Co., 1882), pp. 418–419.
[2] *Ibid.*, p. 372.

5

Is It Worth Losing the World to Save Your Soul?

There is another side to the picture. There are others who chose differently, many others, but for our present purposes I have again chosen three. First, Paul. He was brought up a strict Pharisee and was probably a member of the Jewish Sanhedrin as a comparatively young man. Head and shoulders above his contemporaries as a scholar, his feet were early on the ladder of fame. He hated what he regarded as a heretical sect—the young Church of Christ—and deemed it his duty to oppose it. This he did ruthlessly, imprisoning both men and women and sending them to their death. He was present at the martyrdom of Stephen, assenting to his death and indeed holding the garments of those who stoned him. So great was his zeal that he persecuted beyond the boundaries of Palestine even to foreign cities. This young man had the world at his feet. His pedigree was immaculate—a very Pharisee of Pharisees, of the tribe of Benjamin. In his lineage there was nothing to fault. His progress in the religious sphere was rapid and his scholarly fame widespread. Had he not sat at the feet of Gamaliel, that great teacher?

In a critical hour he was confronted with Christ and made a choice which was not only life-changing but which

I might almost say turned out to be world-changing. On his way to Damascus to continue his work of persecution—having received letters from the rulers of the Jews giving his authority to that end—he met Christ. I love to envisage the scene. I imagine a cloud of dust rising in the desert as the cavalcade comes into view. I picture Paul, or Saul as he then was, riding ahead, urging his horse on with his zeal to get ahead with his work. Suddenly he is down, right off the horse and down on the desert sand. 'He fell,' as one has beautifully put it, 'alive at the feet of Christ.' He saw a light brighter than the noonday sun and He heard a voice, sweeter than the voice of the sons of men: 'Saul, Saul, why persecutest thou Me?' (Acts 9:5)

Blinded by the great light he was led by the hand into Damascus. There, through the laying on of the hands of Ananias, he received his sight and was baptised in the Holy Spirit. He made a choice—the choice to abandon his old way of life and follow the Christ.

Where did it lead him, and did it profit him? His choice led him to isolation in the desert, being prepared for his great life work. It led him into conflict with his erstwhile friends and colleagues. It led him into acute physical danger. On one occasion about forty of his enemies banded themselves together with a solemn oath neither to eat nor drink until they had taken his life. It led him to arduous missionary journeys, to perils on land and sea, to lashings. Tied to poles he received thirty-nine stripes five times. These were laid on the shoulders and chest and would cut to the bone. The wounds afterwards had salt rubbed into them. He was left for dead outside the gates of Lystra—it seems likely that it was on this occasion that he was caught up to the third heaven and heard and saw things which he might not divulge; he was unsure as to whether he was in or out of the body at the time. In any case he suddenly got up and walked away, no doubt to the amazement and discomfiture of his enemies. Dead men are not supposed to get up and walk away. He knew shipwreck, he knew privation and hunger. He knew bonds and imprisonment. He had a terrible time.

In addition to all this he carried on his spirit a constant burden for the churches. He could write, 'My little children, of whom I am again in travail until Christ be formed in you' (Gal 4:19). And he never forgot his early days. The memory of weeping Christians for whose imprisonment and death he had been earlier responsible probably lived with him endlessly and may well have goaded him on to greater endeavour for Christ:

> Saints, did I say? with your remembered faces,
> Dear men and women, whom I sought and slew!
> Ah when we mingle in the heavenly places
> How will I weep to Stephen and to you!
>
> Oh for the strain that ran to our reviling
> Still, when the bruised limbs sank upon the sod,
> Oh for the eyes that looked their last in smiling,
> Last on this world here, but their first on God![1]

For the sake of his people he would have forfeited his own salvation if this could have been the means of winning them: 'For I could wish that I myself were anathema from Christ for my brethren's sake' (Rom 9:3).

He had a thorn in the flesh, we know not what (it may have been an eye defect, or an impediment of speech or some other disability), and God did not remove it but let him know that it was for his good and that His grace was sufficient for him. The thorn kept him very dependent on God and from weakness strength flowed, until he could say that he gloried in his infirmities: 'When I am weak, then am I strong.'

I sometimes imagine a twentieth century follower of Christ seeking an ecclesiastical post and our listening to the interview. 'Well, there is no salary; you can work as Paul did with your own hands (he made tents). No, there are no holidays and no house provided. No, you won't need a house for you will be travelling endlessly and when you are not travelling or living temporarily with the converts you make, you will be in prison. Your life will constantly be in danger.' How many of us would leap at the position?

Now did he really have a terrible time? Indubitably, from one point of view; but from another quite the reverse. I wonder if there was a happier man in history than the apostle Paul. I feel that joy attended all his way. 'I have learned,' he said, 'in whatsoever state I am, therein to be content.' 'Rejoice in the Lord alway: and again I say, Rejoice.' Paul had no self pity. You never find him complaining of his lot in dejection and despair. He was a man of fire and energy, carrying a flaming message across a wicked world, indifferent to his own comfort if by any means he might save some. The longer you ponder his life and the deeper you read the Word, the more does the conviction grow that this man was supremely happy. He had a great time, a tremendous time.[2] He lived dangerously—he lived excitingly—he lived gloriously. 'For I am persuaded,' he wrote, 'that neither death, nor life, nor angels, nor principalities, nor things present, nor things to come, nor powers, nor height, nor depth, nor any other creature, shall be able to separate us from the love of God, which is in Christ Jesus our Lord' (Rom 8:38–39). Not only with patience but with zest he ran the race that was set before him that he might attain the prize.

I see him there with indomitable spirit, head erect, proud of Christ, forging ever forward. Paul, has it been worth it? The road you have taken, the life you have lost and the life you have chosen? I imagine Paul triumphantly proclaiming, 'Had I ten thousand lives I would gladly lay them all down for Jesus.'

One of the things that most potently drew me personally to Christ was the evidence of joy I found in the lives of Christians who lived sacrifically for God, such as the three I have chosen for this study: Hudson Taylor, C.T. Studd and Paul himself. It seemed to me that this joy was a powerful witness to the truth of Christianity. The catechism states: 'Man's chief end is to glorify God and enjoy Him forever.' There should be joy—glorious joy. Instinctively I felt the truth of this. I argued that the religion which produced this was the true religion and I have found it to be indeed so.[3]

Paul lost his life and found it. 'For whosoever would save his life shall lose it,' said Christ, 'and whosoever shall lose his life for my sake and the gospel's shall save it' (Mark 8:35).

What did it profit Paul to take the road he took? Everything—in time and in eternity.

May I ask you, reader, to consider the question seriously: 'For what doth it profit a man, to gain the whole world, and forfeit his soul?'

This question comes immediately after the other, 'What shall I do with Jesus Who is called Christ?' It is as though Christ faces you with your decision regarding Him but allows you to pause and consider the consequence of a mistaken choice, a foolish bargain. Weigh the issues well.

Shall we, as we did at the close of the last chapter, look into the world to come. Remember the scene as Mr Valiant-for-Truth reached the other side in Bunyan's allegory. 'All the trumpets sounded for him.' Remember what the old Chinaman said as he looked at the dead face of Hudson Taylor when the room seemed full of the presence of God: 'Myriads of angels have welcomed him.' What think you of Paul's entrance to the glory? Surely you hear the words, 'Thou good and faithful servant, enter thou into the joy of thy Lord'—and can I hear a faint echo (and perchance not so faint), 'Lord, I have been in your joy for years. For me to live was Christ—to die is gain. Indeed, "what shall it profit a man, to gain the whole world, and forfeit his soul?" For me to lose the world has been endless gain.'

Hudson Taylor, the founder of the China Inland Mission, found that he too had critical choices to make. See him there, a young man who after earlier agnosticism had found Christ. His was no vague discipleship. He had taken Christ as Lord as well as Saviour and now a life-changing, and one might even say a nation-changing, decision is upon him. Before his birth his godly mother had dedicated him to God for China—a land almost wholly unevangelised and teeming with millions of souls. After conversion Hudson, without knowing of his mother's commitment, felt the draw himself and began to prepare for the work, but there was a major obstacle. (There often is in lives deeply called of God.) His fiancée was totally unwilling to go to China. It was clear that he was an acceptable suitor—but his proposed career she was not prepared to share. You can imagine the scene as he went before God. What would it profit him to gain the lady of his heart and lose his call? By God's grace he made the right choice. He refused to forego his life work and stay at home, and today untold millions are in the Glory as a direct or indirect consequence of that choice.

As you see Hudson Taylor in difficulty after difficulty, in danger of life and limb, in danger on land and at sea, you see an indomitable spirit constantly putting Christ first. As he deepened in experience he became increasingly God-dependent. He knew privation; he knew pain and sorrow; he lived dangerously—and yet through that life there came a constant emanation of the peace of God, an emanation of Christ, a serenity, a happiness. The quality of his joy perhaps did more than anything else of its kind to draw me as a young man to Christ. I found the evidence of such joy convincing. This flows from lives who live sacrificially for God.

God blessed him richly, although the path was stony and the way very narrow. No doubt his feet were often bleeding—but his spirit soared into the heavenlies and he walked with God. His work, often vigorously opposed by other missionaries and sometimes by the world generally, was blessed of God. His methods, such as dressing like the people amongst whom he worked, were strongly censured. His marriage to Maria Dyer was bitterly opposed. I could list, as with Paul, many a difficulty, many a sadness, but over all there comes a note of triumph and endless glory—of undeniable victory. You see, ultimately millions turned to Christ from that dark land. Gradually he had gained the confidence of much of the Christian world and men and women answered the call of God and went to serve in China. He never appealed for a penny but walked in faith. Millions of pounds came in and in one year alone one thousand missionaries went out in answer to prayer.

What a life! What a privilege! What a call! What a fulfilment! What a word from the old Chinaman as his great chief pastor lay serene in death, 'Myriads of angels have welcomed him!' What a contrast to a Byron and to a Voltaire! He lost this world and gained the world to come but paradoxically in gaining it got the best of this world as well. It is always so.

We turn next to C. T. Studd. Born into a rich upper class English home, young Studd became an outstanding cricketer. From Eton he went to Cambridge and shone at cricket, his chosen sport. He played not only for his university but for England and became one of the greatest batsmen of his day—playing, for example, in the first game of the Ashes against Australia. At the height of his fame the call of God came to him. He had been converted earlier and now he knew the call to the foreign field. He left behind a home, career, a life of sport and the adulation that goes with it, and sailed for China. He served there and later in India. He felt that God asked him to give away his fortune (then £30,000, probably equal to half a million now). This he did, and ultimately because of sickness it seemed his missionary career was over. He felt, however, God calling him to Africa, but no doctor would pass him and no committee would support him—yet he was determined to obey the call. He then decided that for doctor and committee he would have God the Father, God the Son and God the Holy Spirit and that he would take his instructions from Them alone. The first instruction was to go. He went. His health was in ruins. He had no means of support. He left behind him a bedridden wife. He was much criticised by the Christian world—but he went. On the boat to Africa God spoke again and told him that this venture was not for Africa alone but for the whole unevangelised world. He believed God and laboured in Africa for twenty years. The man who should have died became known as 'the graveyard deserter.' The Africans came by the tens of thousands to Christ. A strong work was established. He wrote to his wife to get up from her sickbed by faith and take charge of the home end of the work, which she did, and did most effectively.

Surely you will say he must have been satisfied. Indeed he was not. The quality of Christianity which in many cases was emerging was far too light for his taste and he raised high the banner of holiness and sanctification and was extremely critical of mere 'believism.' 'Without holiness,' he strongly proclaimed, 'no man shall see God.' It split the movement but he never yielded. He never lowered the standard by a hair-breadth and God honoured him and He honoured the mission.

Like many of God's pioneers he was a terrible man. He had a burning zeal and he expected all other Christians to share that zeal. Life in Christ was a glorious adventure and he expected others to be thrilled as he was thrilled. He was a born leader but he was not always easy to follow. I remember talking to a missionary who knew him well and had worked closely with him. 'He would be up in the morning early before daybreak to be with God and then we might be building a church—we would be on the roof at first light and we stayed there. Dinner time came and I would hope to go down then—but there was no time to go down. He was so taken up with what he was doing that he drove himself on relentlessly and he drove others too. He was a wonderful man—but he was a terrible man.' He expected bravery in his missionaries. He expected them to get food as they went into new areas—if only from the fruits of the forest. If they were in danger and died in the cause they were to rejoice. It was promotion from the front line!

Right to the end he suffered painfully in his body but his spirit was indomitable. He loved his wife but endured long years of separation willingly for Christ's sake. At their last meeting in Africa it was obvious to them that they would never meet again on earth, but he went on—he stayed in Africa and she, with a breaking heart and a brave soul, went back to England to continue the work. For both it was a fearful wrench but for Christ's sake they made the sacrifice. He was prepared to endure hardship as a good soldier of Jesus Christ. He accepted the principle of sacrifice and his motto has lived through all the years: 'If Jesus Christ be God and died for me then no sacrifice that I can make for Him can be too great.'

Like Hudson Taylor's, Studd's was a faithful work. He never appealed for money and yet God met his own need and the needs of the mission. His call indeed proved to be not to the heart of Africa alone but to the whole unevangelised world and today Worldwide Evangelization Crusade, which he founded, has missionaries worldwide. God proved his faithfulness to his servant. Yes he knew privation and pain, bitter opposition and at times almost hatred. He stressed the qualities of courage and heroism and held much of the Church up to ridicule on these counts. He scandalised many by his 'DCD' tract. He often ploughed a lonely furrow but again, as you study his life, there is left an overall impression of victory, joy, glory, overcoming. You feel that despite all the difficulties he had a glorious, fulfilling time. You cannot possibly be sorry for him. When you view the success of his work you humbly bow your head. Like Paul and Hudson Taylor he made the wise choice. He lost the world and found incalculable gain.

Let us view these three lives again. Surely they suffered deeply and lived sacrifically, but who would dare be sorry for them? They obviously lived gloriously and happily. Their lives were surely triumphant and they all proclaim the greatness of the God they served. Indeed they powerfully attract others to follow their example.

'For what shall it profit a man, to gain the whole world, and forfeit his soul?'

What did it profit them to lose the world? Everything—not only did they gain the world to come but they really got the best of this world as well. How do their lives compare with a Judas, a Byron, a Voltaire? Putting these together, even for comparison, seems almost like blasphemy—such a vast span separates them. I leave the reader to draw his own conclusions. I have always regarded this question, 'For what shall it profit a man, to gain the whole world, and forfeit his soul?' as one of the most important that has ever been asked on earth. Remember, it was asked and is still asked by Christ. From everyone He awaits an answer.

Notes

[1] F. W. Myers, *Saint Paul*.

[2] C. T. Studd once wrote of some of the great heroes of faith in cricketing terms, and I seem to remember that he depicted Paul batting and having a wonderful time, a long and glorious innings. The time came, Studd reckoned, for him to move over and let other adventurous souls have a go!

[3] Through many years C. S. Lewis had from time to time had glimpses of insight into truth which reacted on his spirit as almost indefinable joy. It is significant that he named the book in which he described his finding of God, *Surprised by Joy*.

6

Do the Dead Live Again?

I can imagine a reader saying, 'I have followed carefully all you have said about Christ and the witness of good men to Him and I am impressed by Him—profoundly impressed. I realise the importance of the question, "What shall it profit a man, to gain the world and forfeit his own soul?" but I have fundamental doubts about resurrection and the afterlife. I have seen death and find it very difficult to believe that the dead can live again or that Christ really did rise from the dead. I accept that miracles happen, that life is itself a miracle; but with this particular miracle I find it very difficult to come to terms.'

Your problem I fully understand and once faced it myself. The words of Paul sound in my ear—'How are the dead raised? and with what manner of body do they come?'

I want to face you with a startling truth that few people seem to realise. The body you yourself now have was not in existence seven years ago and scarce a cell of it will remain seven years from now. Within this period almost every particle passes away. In other words a man of seventy has had ten totally different bodies and yet his identity remains; his various changing bodies have looked alike. Does it become so impossible to believe that in a coming day God could give him yet another body which will perfectly fit his identity?

In 1 Corinthians 15 Paul speaks much of the resurrection of the dead and bases his argument on two fundamental points. Firstly, nature itself teaches that resurrection goes on all the time; and secondly, Christ rose from the dead. I would like to deal with both points.

In nature a grain of wheat is planted, it 'dies' in the ground and from it a plant grows with perhaps a hundred new ears. It died and in a sense rose again. We witness the miracle year after year in the harvest fields. We expect it to happen. When the farmer plants his fields he plants with the expectation of harvest. It is a law of nature and if that law failed humanity would die of starvation, and yet it is a miracle. Year after year it happens and we take it for granted. Nevertheless it *is* a miracle. God has so programmed seed (if I may use such an expression) that, combined with soil and weather, after it dies there will be new life born—it is in nature the miracle of resurrection.

Paul's main argument, however, is the resurrection of Christ Himself. He, like all the early Church, considered this fundamental to the doctrine of Christianity. What is the evidence?

Let me say at the outset that the resurrection of Christ is one of the best authenticated facts of ancient history. The case is irrefutable. Consider some of the salient points:

1. Christ accurately predicted His death, the length of time His body would be in the grave and the fact that He would then rise again.

2. His enemies knew of this prediction and either because they feared its fulfilment or that His body might be stolen, secured the co-operation of the Roman authorities to have the tomb sealed by a great stone and guarded by soldiers during the critical period. Despite this

He came out of the tomb at the predicted time and no man was ever able to produce His dead body to refute His disciples' claim that he had risen from the dead.

3. The Bible tells us that the Jews bribed the soldiers to say that Christ's disciples had stolen the body while they slept. This is peculiarly ridiculous. It was more than a Roman soldier's life was worth to sleep on guard duty and, secondly, sleeping men make very unconvincing witnesses as to what has happened while they have inhabited the world of dreams.

4. We are told that during a period of forty days Jesus showed Himself alive by many infallible proofs. There are many recorded appearances from which the following is a selection. We read that He was seen first by Mary Magdalene and later by other women, by Peter and by the gathered apostles, on one occasion without Thomas and then with Thomas, by two disciples on the Emmaus road and by his apostles at and before His ascension.

5. Paul adds to this that He was seen by himself, as one born out of due time, and by more than five hundred brethren at one time 'of whom the greater part,' he wrote, 'remain until now,' i.e., were alive at the time of writing.

6. The New Testament account has a very authentic ring. The writers and the early Church generally do not come out of the matter with credit. Christ had plainly foretold events. They had either disregarded Him or disbelieved Him. From deepest gloom they were surprised into life with His resurrection. It obviously came as an unexpected shock. The surprise is there for all to feel in the written pages. There is no note of doubt as to the fact at any point in the narrative. Indeed there are two quite remarkable cases where previous doubt is banished.

First, when two of His followers walked to Emmaus they spoke of the events around the crucifixion. Christ Himself, unrecognised by them, drew near and walked with them. They lamented His death, having hoped that it was He Who would redeem Israel. They had no doubt that He was dead and obviously no thought that he would rise again. While their hearts 'burned within them' as He talked on the way, they still did not recognise Him. Not until He broke bread in the house did they become aware of His identity and then there was such a certainty that they immediately went back to Jerusalem to convey the news in spite of the lateness of the hour. The story rings remarkably true.

The second case is that of Thomas and it is a very convincing story. Absent when Christ appeared to the rest of the apostles, he heard of the matter and spoke words whose strength and bitterness have echoed down all the years: 'Except I shall see in his hands the print of the nails, and put my finger into the print of the nails, and put my hand into his side, I will not believe.' Many a reader of the New Testament has empathised with Thomas. I see him there as a man who had given his loyalty and trust to Christ and had felt desperately disillusioned at His death. He saw the One he had believed to be the Son of God dead on a cross—indisputably dead. How could it be? He had declared Himself to be the Messiah, the Son of God, but He was dead! Did blasphemous thoughts rise in the mind of Thomas regarding the veracity of Christ? We do not know all that went through the minds of the followers of Christ in those dark hours. Were their hopes crushed, buried with Him in a borrowed tomb? Christ in the garden had warned Peter, James and John to watch and pray that they might not enter into temptation. Little did they realise that not only was the crisis of Christ upon Him but their own great crisis hours were upon them and they were unprepared, and little did they realise the truth of the words Christ was so soon to utter to others, 'This is your hour and the power of darkness.' The position of these early disciples must have been horrendous. They had believed Him to be the Son of God and confessed it. Under

Mosaic law to attribute deity to a mere man was punishable by death and no doubt put the immortal soul in jeopardy for the life to come. To be mistaken in such a matter had momentous consequences and to all outward appearance they had been mistaken—desperately mistaken. The gloom that fell on Peter and the others is almost tangible in the Scriptures—as is the wondrous joy that accompanied the resurrection. 'He is alive!' It rippled like music and intoxicated like new wine. It was a new dawn on earth and they fully entered into it.

But back to Thomas: he was a worthy representative of an attitude that many may have shared, although his may have been an extreme position. 'Except I shall see in his hands the print of the nails, and put my finger into the print of the nails, and put my hand into his side, I will not believe' (Jn 20:25). Do I hear him say in the language of his time the equivalent of: 'I have been conned once, I will not be conned again. I am having no fancy stories or vain hopeful imaginations. I will not be duped in any way. I will not only see with my eyes but I will touch with my hands before I believe again.' Stout words, strong resolves; not a bitter blasphemer but a broken man who needs a sure foundation, an absolutely sure foundation before he trusts again. With this man we can empathise. We understand this man. And indeed in a sense we thank God for him because his attitude led to a particular encounter with Christ which provides powerful evidence for the reality of the physical resurrection of our Lord.

> And after eight days again his disciples were within, and Thomas with them. Jesus cometh, the doors being shut, and stood in the midst, and said, Peace be unto you. Then saith he to Thomas, Reach hither thy finger, and see my hands; and reach hither thy hand, and put it into my side: and be not faithless, but believing. Thomas answered and said unto him, My Lord and my God. Jesus saith unto him, Because thou

> hast seen me, thou hast believed: blessed are they that have not seen, and yet have believed (Jn 20:26–29).

It is so dignified, so convincing. Few can read the passage without being struck with both the drama and its ring of truth.

The appearance of Christ to Mary Magdalene in the garden immediately after His resurrection is also highly convincing. Had the gospel writer been trying to concoct a story one would have expected instant recognition as one might have done with the two on the Emmaus road, but we are plainly told that Mary supposed Him to be the gardener. Neither she, nor the eleven, expected to see Him. They were all convinced He was dead. It is a common occurrence in life to fail to recognise a known person immediately when we meet them out of context. We often have to look twice before recognition is full. So it was with Mary. It may be that something familiar in the voice caught her attention when He spoke her name. She may at first only have seen the form without looking at the face. In any case the record is wholly convincing.

The writers of the New Testament do not shield themselves in any way. Their failure and unbelief are freely acknowledged. Their writings are not the writings of men who have fabricated a story.

Paul's reference to the company of over five hundred who saw Christ at one time and the majority of whom were still alive when he wrote is particularly significant. This was a statement that was being made publicly; it went down in writing; it could be challenged. Who were they? Paul left himself totally open to this and quite evidently had no fear of an investigation. This is evidence of a critical nature.

If we stand back from the canvas for a little and look from an objective position an extremely convincing picture emerges:

A company of people who saw Christ crucified and buried and had no hope of seeing Him in this life again became totally convinced that He rose from the dead. The report states that He appeared to hundreds of them and talked with them on numerous occasions, and that He demonstrated that He was not a spirit by being handled and by partaking of food. So sure were they of His resurrection that they proclaimed it openly and indeed held its truth as a cornerstone of their faith. For this many were put to death. That they were totally convinced of the resurrection and prepared to die for it is indisputable from the records. It would be odd if a body of people whose teaching so emphasised integrity and honestly had fabricated a story, spread a lie and gone on to die for it. We just cannot accept this.

It is interesting too that the resurrection is first proclaimed in the city outside whose walls the crucifixion took place. A man might tell of wonders in a far land of which he had heard from a friend of a friend of a relative. Such testimony usually carries little weight. In a court of law hearsay is not evidence. Had the resurrection been first proclaimed in Rome—far from the scene of crucifixion—we might have had cause to doubt; but no, it was proclaimed right in the city of Jerusalem and, let me say it again, proclaimed at the peril of the lives of those who did so. For it they endured torture, imprisonment and death. Would they have done this for a known lie? Hardly! And in addition to all this I would again emphasise that the enemies of Christ were never able to produce His dead body, and that, despite the fact that they had taken measures to prevent its removal from the tomb—strong measures: an official Roman Guard. Do you realise that the dead body of Christ was never produced either then or later? All that the enemies required to do at any point to kill all thought of His resurrection was to produce His dead body. It was never done, for it was never there. The account in John is lovely:

> Now on the first day of the week cometh Mary Magdalene early, while it was yet dark, unto the tomb, and seeth the stone taken away from the tomb. She runneth therefore, and cometh to Simon Peter, and to the other disciple, whom Jesus loved, and saith unto them, They have taken away the Lord out of the tomb, and we know not where they have laid him. Peter therefore went forth, and the other disciple, and they went toward the tomb. And they ran both together: and the other disciple outran Peter, and came first to the tomb; and stooping and looking in, he seeth the linen cloths lying; yet entered he not in. Simon Peter therefore also cometh, following him, and entered into the tomb; and he beholdeth the linen cloths lying, and the napkin, that was upon his head, not lying with the linen cloths, but rolled up in a place by itself. Then entered in therefore the other disciple also, which came first to the tomb, and he saw, and believed. For as yet they knew not the scripture, that he must rise again from the dead. So the disciples went away again unto their own home.
>
> But Mary was standing without at the tomb weeping: so, as she wept, she stooped and looked into the tomb; and she beholdeth two angels in white sitting, one at the head, and one at the feet, where the body of Jesus had lain. And they say unto her, Woman, why weepest thou? She saith unto them, Because they have taken away my Lord, and I know not where they have laid him. When she had thus said, she turned herself back, and beholdeth Jesus standing, and knew not that it was Jesus. Jesus saith unto her, Woman, why weepest thou? whom seekest thou? She, supposing him to be the gardener, saith unto him, Sir, if thou has borne him hence, tell me where thou hast laid him, and I will take him away. Jesus saith unto her, Mary. She turned herself, and saith unto him in Hebrew, Rabboni; which is to say, Master. Jesus saith to her, Touch me not; for I am not yet ascended unto the Father: but go unto my brethren, and say to them, I ascend unto my Father and your Father, and my God and your God. Mary Magdalene cometh and telleth the disciples, I have seen the

Lord; and how that he had said these things unto her (Jn 20:1–18).

No, the case for the resurrection is irrefutable and as surely as He rose from the dead so shall we, but 'each in his own order.' Christ was the first fruit, then we that are His at His coming, and then the resurrection of the lost.

Let no doubt of the authenticity of the resurrection prevent your coming to Christ.

7

Indeed They Do!

This chapter is more personal and it may strike a chord with readers. I was brought up in a Christian home and taught that there was an afterlife—the soul's destiny being either Heaven or hell. I was familiar with the story of Lazarus and the rich man. I had no doubt of Bible teaching on hell—a place of endless alienation from God and of endless pain, a place where there was memory of the earth life and recollection of past misdeeds, a place where remorse eats like a canker, a place forever divided from the abode of the blest by a great gulf fixed.

I was taught also that there was a Heaven. If there was a hell to shun there was a Heaven to gain. I knew of Christ and the doctrine of salvation. I knew of Christ's resurrection and the promise of resurrection for all men, some to endless life and glory, the remainder to intolerable destruction. I was orthodox in this conservative view and mentally accepted the teaching as being Biblical—and then there came a day!

I was by this time genuinely converted and indeed working for God. At an open air meeting I had met an elderly man who made a profession of salvation and some time after took a stroke. I visited him for about six months until he died. I was not present at the actual time of death but visited the home shortly afterwards. I was invited to see him before interment. Now in Scotland offence may be given by not doing this, so although not particularly wanting to look on death, I went into the room where the body lay in its coffin. I will never forget the experience. I should perhaps say I was no stranger to death. Before I was ten years old I had known the deaths of an aunt and uncle who had lived in our home, then of a deeply loved father and finally of a brother murdered as a young man of twenty-four. I had known death—indeed on the morning I awoke to find a sister weeping at the foot of my bed and hear the words, 'Donald's dead,' I thought something like, 'It's happened again' and scarcely took in the awful truth. Yes, death was known in our home, deeply and sadly known. Indeed, after the death of my brother it seemed to me that a joy went out of my mother's life. When his name was mentioned her lip trembled and after a time we never spoke his name in her presence. She carried her pain for over forty years—dying in her ninety-seventh year.

In spite of all this background, in a sense I met death for the first time in that old man's home. I looked at what was like a death mask of a face. He was dead—he was terribly dead. I was shocked by death as I had never been shocked before and there rose in me, from the depths of my being a doubt that I would ever see him again or any other who had ever died. I suddenly fundamentally doubted life after death and I was shocked at myself and at my unbelief. For a few seconds I stood on that floor with my faith rocking. You may say, 'But did you not believe the Bible?' My friend, there is a difference between a mental assent to a doctrine and a full spiritual conviction of its truth. I was down at a basic level. I might say I believed—but I did not really believe. I fundamentally doubted. That was the truth—unpalatable as it may seem. For a short time I stood as one pole-axed. Then suddenly I thought of Christ. I realised that there had been a day on which He was as dead as was my friend. His face was as dead as the face that had shocked me a few moments earlier. I then realised something of the significance for all men of Christ's resurrection. I am a historian by profession and evidence has always been important to me. I realised the unassailable case for Christ's own resurrection. It really is one of the best authenticated facts of ancient history. As Wilbur Smith put it: 'Let it simply be said that we know more about the details of the hours immediately before and the actual death of Jesus in and near Jerusalem, than we know about the death of any other one man in all the ancient world.'[1] Suddenly there came over me an overwhelming conviction that as Christ rose so would my friend, so would I, so would all men. The resurrection of Christ is indeed a veritable cornerstone, a foundation of faith. Never again have I had doubt about life after death.

Since then I have gone more deeply into the spiritual dimension. I have known the ministry of angels and heard the voice of God, and any earlier vague belief in resurrection is replaced by an absolute conviction both of this and of the world to come. Indeed the world to come becomes more real than the present material world.

'Yes,' you may say, 'that is your belief, your experience, your testimony, but have you nothing more to add by way of objective evidence?' As it happens I do—much more!

A number of years ago I was speaking to a far-out relative who spoke of a wonderful experience in her earlier life. She is a lady of great integrity who was consistently engaged in the work of God in her active years. (She is an old lady now.) While spiritual, she was a 'douce Scots buddy' (if you know the term) with two feet firmly planted on the ground. An hour came when her mother lay dying. She watched alone by the bedside. As the end drew near it was as though a light shone on her mother's face. She evidently saw something wonderful. The daughter knelt by the bed in a state of desolation. She was an only daughter and her attachment to her mother was particularly deep. She said, 'I felt I could not go on living if my mother was taken.' She didn't mean she would take her own life or anything like that—but simply that the tie was so deep that she could not live without her mother. Suddenly, she said, as she knelt there the room was filled with angelic presence and angelic music filled the air. Quite clearly she heard an angel choir and she followed the words of their song—words she had never heard or read (although she did find them later):

> O call it not death: it is life begun,
> For the waters are passed and the harbour is won.

Again and again the refrain was repeated, one voice seeming to lead the others. The room was full of the sound, which ultimately took on a jubilant note:

> O call it not death: it is life begun,
> For the waters are passed and the harbour is won.

The power and the joy of it, she said, entered her being. She thrilled in response. 'I knew,' she said, 'that when I rose from my knees the visitation would end, but ultimately I had to let my brothers know of my mother's death and it did end—but I rose from my knees, not to die but to live for Christ.' This she did faithfully for many years.

Another of my friends speaks of a light shining so brightly on her dying grandmother's face that an uncle turned to tell whoever had the torch to put it out—but that torch was never lit on earth.

Through the years it has been my privilege and duty to be present at many deathbeds. I have seen fear banished as the presence of God has come in such an hour. I have known the coming of real vision as death drew near. There is a God-given ministry for the death chamber and the glory of God shines brightly there.

One of my own most memorable experiences of this type occurred when a highly respected Christian from Kilsyth in Scotland, a Mr Jack, went home. I knew the family well and waited at the bedside. As the end came I suddenly felt myself go out with him in an ecstacy, right, I felt, to the very gates and maybe even a little way inside. The glory was unspeakable. I found myself spontaneously prophesying and glorifying God. Call it death? It was life eternal, glorious life. Death for such a man was but the portal, the ante-room of Heaven. Well might Paul declare:

> Nay, in all these things we are more than conquerors through him that loved us. For I am persuaded, that neither death, nor life, nor angels, nor principalities, nor things present, nor things to come, nor powers, nor height, nor depth, nor any other creature, shall be able to separate us from the love of God, which is in Christ Jesus our Lord (Rom 8:37–39).

I was with a Mr Jauncey of Falkirk when he too passed away and at his funeral service the glory of God fell and it was as though a voice from eternity spoke to a great company of mourners. The glory of God was there. I could instance funeral after funeral where this kind of thing has happened. You may find it strange to read that I often prefer funerals to weddings. At the former there is reality and God is there. Too often at the latter there is over-much frivolity and unreality. Unsanctified human nature and artificiality too often take the stage.

One final case: that of the late Mr Gault of Ballymena in Ireland. In his life he walked with God. He was a deep man of God. I had the privilege of being with him as he left the body. Again and again the Word spoke to him before the end and his was a triumphant passing. His funeral of which I write in *Reflections on the Gifts of the Spirit* was an outstanding occasion. The power and the glory of God fell and few who were there are likely to forget it.

Yes, I believe in the power of the world to come. I believe in the resurrection of Christ and in the resurrection of all men.

May I conclude with a story I first heard many years ago—a true story, which has affected many people. I quote from Michael Green, who writes:

> ...two able young men, Gilbert West and Lord Lyttleton, went up to Oxford. They were friends of Dr Johnson and Alexander Pope, in the swim of society. They were determined to attack the very basis of the Christian faith. So Lyttleton settled down to prove that Saul of Tarsus was never converted to Christianity, and West to demonstrate that Jesus never rose from the tomb.
>
> Some time later, they met to discuss their findings. Both were a little sheepish. For they had come independently to similar and disturbing conclusions. Lyttleton found, on examination, that Saul of Tarsus *did* become a radically new man through his conversion to Christianity; and West found that the evidence pointed unmistakably to the fact that Jesus did rise from the dead. You may still find his book in a large library. It is entitled *Observations on the History and Evidences of the Resurrection of Jesus Christ*, and was published in 1747.[2] On the fly-leaf he has had printed his telling quotation from Ecclesiasticus 11:7, which might be adopted with profit by any modern agnostic: *"Blame not before thou hast examined the truth."*[3]

Finally, the testimony of millions of Christians through the ages is quite simply that apart from Christ's appearances in the days of the early Church and throughout the years, He has come to live and does live in the hearts and lives of His humblest followers. Come and taste for yourself, my reader friends.

Notes

[1] Josh McDowell, *Evidence That Demands a Verdict*, p. 186, quoting Wilbur M. Smith, *Therefore Stand: Christian Apologetics* (Baker Book House, 1965).

[2] For readers interested in pursuing this theme see Frank Morison, *Who Moved the Stone?* (Faber and Faber, 1967).

[3] McDowell, *op. cit*, p. 193.

8

Christ the Revolutionary

I can hear a reader, and particularly a young reader, say, 'I must acknowledge that the case you make for resurrection is indeed strong, and the picture you present of Christ attractive, but I feel I am meeting in your writing a very different Christ from the one that is popularly imagined. Why is this?'

Throughout much of a lifetime it has been my privilege and my job to deal with youth and occasionally I think I was able to see the world, at least to some extent, through their eyes—and the picture they often had of Christ and the Church I fear was shocking.

Are we not to blame? Somehow there has got abroad a caricature of Christ—a stained-glass window picture of a weak, anaemic person—a milk and water character continually dropping soft and smooth words. The Church is regarded as particularly anaemic, an institution hiding a deal of hypocrisy—an effete, outdated establishment.

This is terrible! Have a true look at the real Christ and the Church as He conceived it.

He was brought up in Nazareth, a village noted for its sinfulness—partly because it was located on a trade route. There, in obscurity, He probably learned Joseph's trade of carpentry. At about the age of thirty He became an itinerant teacher leading a small band of disciples around the country. His message was unique. He demanded repentance as did John the Baptist, His forerunner. This was His opening message. He demanded that men get right in their attitude to God. He taught absolute righteousness in all human dealings and total submission to the rule of God. This meant accepting Him as the Son of God, the Sent One. He demanded total allegiance of the human heart and promised to meet the deepest needs of man. 'Follow Me,' He said to His first disciples. 'Take My yoke upon you,' He said on another occasion, and again, 'Except ye believe in Me ye shall die in your sins.'

On 'the last day, the great day of the feast,' we read that He stood and cried, 'If any man thirst, let him come unto me, and drink.' To the woman at the well He said, 'If thou knewest the gift of God, and who it is that saith to thee, Give me to drink; thou wouldest have asked of him and he would have given thee living water.' What statements! Imagine any man standing and promising to satisfy all human thirst! It was staggering in its conception and promise.

One of the most noticeable features about Christ's preaching was its uncompromising nature. His principles never altered and His standards never lowered. He taught total obedience to the will of His Father. He pointed men to perfection—nothing less than the will of God was acceptable. He taught that man could be changed, could be born again, could live in a way that was well-pleasing to God. He did not suggest that this would be without cost. Indeed, He never made a suggestion nor expressed an opinion. He gave commands and made absolute statements, teaching as One having authority and not as the scribes, whose teaching was so often tentative. He recognised the cost of following Him—which was to lose this present life in exchange for the life to come: 'He that findeth his life shall lose it; and he that loseth his life for my sake shall find it,' and 'If any man would come after me, let him deny himself, and take up his cross, and follow me.' He realised that this could disrupt family and social life. 'He that loveth father or mother more than me is not worthy of me; and he that loveth son or daughter more than me is not worthy of me.' He demanded the first allegiance of the human heart, and not only did He demand it, but such is His power that in a multitude of cases He has received it.

You will realise that inevitably a person with such an uncompromising message would clash with the world He found around Him. He was born in an age when the Jews were under Roman rule although they had their own despised King, Herod, who was really a dissolute and subservient lackey of Rome. The Roman yoke does not appear to have been over-severe in Christ's day. Certainly she demanded and received taxes but over all left the Jews with a good deal of liberty and certainly religious liberty—although the power to put to death for the infringement of the Mosaic law was no longer theirs. Hence we observe the clash developing not so much with the Romans as with His own people. His teaching of absolute righteousness and condemnation of all forms of hypocrisy were calculated to produce total opposition and hatred.

The two main parties amongst the Jews were the Pharisees and the Sadducees. The latter were materialistic in outlook and, while generally orthodox, believed neither in angels nor in the resurrection; the Pharisees, on the other hand, were often bigoted in their rigid religion. This was based on Moses and the prophets, but their system had distorted true and acceptable teaching almost out of recognition. In addition to the law of Moses there had developed a body of oral law carrying almost equal weight. Comment of rabbis through the ages had acquired an authority. In short, a rigid system had arisen where truth was distorted and legalism reigned. The distance a man might walk on the sabbath day, for example, was precisely defined. The rubbing together of ears of corn for food by such a traveller was defined as work and as such forbidden. Evidently, according to tradition, there were even debates about such foolish questions as to how many angels might stand on the point of a needle. Now, while insisting on the observance of the minutiae of the Law such as the tithing of mint and anise and cummin and the ritualistic cleansing of platters, many of the Pharisees failed to observe 'the weightier matters of the law, judgment, and mercy, and faith.'

Into this situation Christ burst disruptively. He saw through to the heart of its hypocrisy and lifted His voice like a trumpet. With an sevenfold woe He denounced the Pharisees. He had observed how they loved the chief places at feasts. He observed that they loved to wear broad phylacteries on their foreheads (marks of supposed piety) and say long prayers at street corners where others would see them. He pointed out that they were very ready to lay heavy burdens on others but were unwilling to lift a finger to help to lighten or carry the burdens. He exposed their hypocrisy over sabbath observance by showing how in what they considered to be emergency they were quite prepared to work as, for example, if one of their animals fell into a ditch and was in danger.

Over the years Christ had discomfited them. They tried to trap Him with cleverly devised questions as, for example, over the paying of tribute to Rome. 'Is it lawful,' they asked, 'to do this?' Had He said 'Yes,' they would have held Him up to the scorn of the people as being unpatriotic and subservient to Rome—no true Messiah. Had He said 'No,' they would have reported Him to Rome for sedition. What did He say? Simply, 'Show me the tribute money.' When the penny was produced He asked, 'Whose is this image and superscription?' 'Caesar's,' they replied. 'Render therefore unto Caesar the things that are Caesar's; and unto God the things that are God's.' By accepting Caesar's coinage they had already tacitly accepted his sovereignty. 'Give Caesar back his own,' He said, 'but don't forget to give to God what is due to Him.' Brilliantly He then reversed the position. 'I would ask you a question. The baptism of John, was it from Heaven or of men?' So simple the question seems to us but to them it was devastating. They were religious leaders and were expected by the people to know about such matters and this put them on the horns of a fearful dilemma. If they said, 'From men,' they might have been torn in pieces by the crowd who, by this time, regarded martyred John as a prophet (this often happens after a prophet is dead). If they said, 'From Heaven,' He was in a position to say, 'Why then did you not believe him, for he testified of Me and recognised My Messiahship.' This they had not done, nor dreamed of doing, so they were forced to the ignominious position of saying, 'We do not know'—and that, in front of all the people. On such a fundamental point the religious leaders were ignorant. How they must have slunk away from that encounter, and we read the significant words, 'From that day durst no man ask him any questions.' From boyhood I have always found that disappointing. His answers were so brilliant, so wonderfully satisfying.

However, as He came nearer the end of His ministry the great final clash came. He uttered the seven-fold denunciation:

> But woe unto you, scribes and Pharisees, hypocrites! because ye shut the kingdom of heaven against men: for ye enter not in yourselves, neither suffer ye them that are entering in to enter....
>
> Woe unto you, scribes and Pharisees, hypocrites! for ye compass sea and land to make one proselyte; and when he is become so, ye make him twofold more a son of hell than yourselves.

Woe unto you, ye blind guides, which say, Whosoever shall swear by the temple, it is nothing; but whosoever shall swear by the gold of the temple, he is a debtor. Ye fools and blind: for whether is greater, the gold, or the temple that hath sanctified the gold?...

Woe unto you, scribes and Pharisees, hypocrites! for ye tithe mint and anise and cummin, and have left undone the weightier matters of the law, judgement, and mercy, and faith: but these ye ought to have done, and not to have left the other undone. Ye blind guides, which strain out the gnat, and swallow the camel.

Woe unto you, scribes and Pharisees, hypocrites! for ye cleanse the outside of the cup and of the platter, but within they are full from extortion and excess. Thou blind Pharisee, cleanse first the inside of the cup and of the platter, that the outside thereof may become clean also.

Woe unto you, scribes and Pharisees, hypocrites! for ye are like unto whited sepulchres, which outwardly appear beautiful, but inwardly are full of dead men's bones, and of all uncleanness. Even so ye also outwardly appear righteous unto men, but inwardly ye are full of hypocrisy and iniquity.

Woe unto you, scribes and Pharisees, hypocrites! for ye build the sepulchres of the prophets, and garnish the tombs of the righteous, and say, If we had been in the days of our fathers, we should not have been partakers with them in the blood of the prophets. Wherefore ye witness to yourselves, that ye are sons of them that slew the prophets. Fill ye up then the measure of your fathers. Ye serpents, ye offspring of vipers, how shall ye escape the judgement of hell? Therefore, behold, I send unto you prophets, and wise men, and scribes: some of them shall ye kill and crucify; and some of them shall ye scourge in your synagogues, and persecute from city to city: that upon you may come all the righteous blood shed on the earth, from the blood of Abel the righteous unto the blood of Zachariah son of Barachiah, whom ye slew between the sanctuary and the altar. Verily I say unto you, All these things shall come upon this generation (Mt 23:13,15–17,23–36).

Note particularly the fearful imagery of the sixth denunciation. He compared the Pharisees to whited sepulchres, no doubt easily imagined by all—outwardly beautiful, gleaming white, but charnel houses inside, full of dead men's bones and putrefaction. What an attack! What perception and what courage to deliver such an anathema! No wonder they hated bitterly. True it might have been; indeed, true it was, but the truth so often devastates much more completely than does a lie or false accusation—and here was the truth. He knew it and they knew it and what probably hurt most was the fact that the people knew it as well.

Note next the words, 'Ye serpents, ye offspring of vipers, how shall ye escape the judgement of hell?' I want you to observe the language. The words are the words of Christ: 'You serpents...children of vipers.' Fearful, awful, reminiscent of John. He too had spoken of them as offspring of vipers. Let me say it bluntly: there was nothing mealy-mouthed about the words of Christ. They could and did cut like a lash when this was required. With a lash He had driven men and cattle out of the Temple when in their materialism and greed the Temple was desecrated. This is the kind of person Christ was. Utterly brave and courageous, totally opposed to hypocrisy, no fear touched His spirit. He carried out the works of God uncompromisingly. And yet He was so gentle and kind that He received the little children gladly and dealt so graciously with the sinful woman at the well and with the woman taken in adultery whom her accusers would have stoned. What a balanced, wonderful personality! No wonder He has drawn men with an irresistible magnetism through the ages.

My chapter heading speaks of Him as Christ the revolutionary. I consider Him to be the world's greatest revolutionary. Some claim, you may say, but how, precisely, can you justify it?

Christ's teachings affect the fabric of every society into which they come. They make supreme demands on nations, on communities, and on individuals. His revolution is a revolution of righteousness and is very costly. It aims at the hearts of men. It does not start with a community or a nation but with individuals. He demands a change in the matter of holiness in every person who comes to Him. This is more costly to the fallen part of our nature than the demands of any other revolutionary leader who ever lived—be it Karl Marx or Che Guevera or Mao Tse-tung. He makes a demand that no other teacher ever made and moreover He expects it to be actually outworked in the everyday affairs of life. It is not a religion for the monastery alone—it is for the highways and byways of life. Outworked consistently it affects not only our relations with God, but also with each other. Not only are we to love Him with all our hearts, but also our neighbours as ourselves, and to love our fellow disciples with Christ's own love—the new commandment He gave (Jn 13:34). It affects our attitude to family life. There is to be love between husbands and wives, between parents and children (by no means universal in non-Christian societies). It affects our attitude to the law of the land, to which we owe obedience provided this does not clash with a deeper law of God. It touches our possessions, all of which are to be held as from God and to be at His disposal as He directs. It affects every aspect of life.

In the wider community the law of Christ has something to say about justice and has affected law-making generally and our personal dealings with each other. It forever remembers the poor and the deprived. Through the ages it has affected our institutions, our legal systems, our provision for the sick as, for example, in the building of hospitals. It affected the ending of the slave trade and also of slavery. It dealt with prison reform and with education. Its influence is pervasive. Everywhere that river flows there is healing.

Whether it deals with the individual as with the rich young ruler who was unwilling to give his all and follow Christ, or with a nation, it is uncompromising in its demand. The young man failed to meet it and was sorrowful, for he had great possessions. No doubt Christ saw the idol he had erected in his heart to riches and wanted him free, but He knew that for him to enter into true freedom he would have to let riches go. He tried to help him—not to wound him, but it was too much for the young man who went away sorrowful and was left in his bound condition. Christ neither pursued him nor, so far as we know, ever addressed another word to him. Similarly communities and nations who disregard His law suffer all the consequences of so doing: and is not our community suffering desperately today—aids, drugs, prostitution, violence and murder rampant?

Yes, shall we forget the stained-glass window caricatures of the Son of God and see a man—the God man—the Man Who was different from any other who ever lived. Strong, courageous, brave beyond our knowing, wise, loving, considerate, compassionate, kind—the very Son of God Who was also God the Son.

Such was, indeed such is He, and such does He expect His Church, His followers, to be. Revolution ran like wine through masses of Frenchmen immediately after 1789. It propelled them onwards through the revolutionary wars when they faced almost all of Europe and immediately after, when under Napoleon they almost conquered the world. It ran like fire in the early days of communism in Russia and again in China and in Cuba. Men were moved to their deeps with revolutionary fervour—and for what lesser causes.

'Oh yes,' you may say, 'but they did have in these later cases a good goal—a redistribution of wealth and greater equality.' Basically it added up to the redistribution of others' wealth and it does not tend to endure. Christ puts His hand first on *your* wealth not your neighbour's. You are not asked to grab that of others but to distribute your own. His is not a revolution of force, torture, imprisonment, but of love and Christlike service for others.

Revolution also sometimes runs like fire through other religions—take Mohammed and various holy wars of the Muslim. With fire and sword they devastated lands and subjected nations. Christ harms none. Neither by force nor sword does He make converts yet He has captivated the hearts of untold millions and where His kingdom goes justice goes, love goes, mercy goes, God goes.

Does your being not instinctively rise to His challenge? You say, 'But the picture you present of His kingdom is not the picture I see when I look at the Church now or through the ages.' No, the Church has much to answer for, but when it, or any part of it, has fully obeyed Christ, my picture stands, and there are churches, and there have been churches throughout the ages, who have followed the way of holiness and reaped the rewards of so doing. 'This is the way, walk ye in it!'

Finally, let me say again that in my days as a Headmaster I was brought into very close contact with young people. I found that the stained-glass window picture had no appeal—the sickly presentation of Christ drew none—but I did notice that when He was presented as He is, He drew like a magnet and many responded to that call. He was a Man Whom they could proudly follow and by God's grace many of them did just that. What of my present readers? Do you catch the drumbeat—feel the iron of Christ and find in Him a leader to follow to the ends of the earth, to the very gates of Hell and finally through the gates of Heaven? I have never regretted my choice. I am proud of my commander and thoroughly recommend you to enlist under His banner, glorious in its crimson red, worthy of the world's greatest revolutionary—but mark, the red speaks not of greed nor acquisition nor of the blood of others but of His own blood, shed for the life of the world.

9

Hell

'There is one thing that sticks in my throat—the doctrine of hell. I just cannot believe that God would allow any of His creatures to go into an eternal fire. The whole idea revolts me. What have you to say about this?'

Perhaps nothing in the teachings of Christ has stirred more controversy than the doctrine of hell. Throughout history it has surfaced powerfully in times of revival and declined in times when spiritual life ebbed low. It has scandalised the minds of men and in many cases met with total rejection, and that sometimes even from Christian leaders. You are not alone in your objections, nor are you the first to voice them.

Let me state the problem quite bluntly at the outset: How can we conceive of a God of love condemning any of His creatures to endless suffering, as the doctrine of hell seems to imply? This may be over-simplistic, but it will provide a basis for approaching the problem.

Prior to Christ's day, the Israelites had very vague and ill-defined ideas about life after death and the destiny of the soul—but Christ gave sharp focus to the whole subject. He spoke far more about hell than He did about Heaven, and indeed the doctrine of hell is almost solely derived from His teaching. His story of the rich man in hell is fundamental to our study, and it is the first focus of our attention.

We read in Luke 16 of two men who lived on earth—one was very rich and he 'fared sumptuously' every day—the other was very poor and he 'ate of the crumbs which fell from the rich man's table, and the dogs licked his sores.' The day came when they both died, and we are baldly told that the rich man lifted up his eyes in hell[1], being in torment, and saw Lazarus afar off in Abraham's bosom[2] and called to him to send Lazarus, that he might 'dip the tip of his finger in water' to cool his parched tongue, 'for,' he said, 'I am in anguish in this flame.' The answer came ringing back, 'Son, remember that thou in thy lifetime receivedst thy good things, and Lazarus in like manner evil things: but now here he is comforted, and thou art in anguish. And beside all this, between us and you there is a great gulf fixed, that they which would pass from hence to you may not be able, and that none may cross over from thence to us' (Lk 16:25–26). The rich man then pled with Abraham to send someone back to earth to warn his five brothers lest they also come to the same place of torment. This was refused with the words, 'They have Moses and the prophets; let them hear them.... If they hear not Moses and the prophets, neither will they be persuaded, if one rise from the dead' (Lk 16:29,31).

Immediately some will say, 'But you can't take this literally. Christ often taught figuratively, and surely this is a parable and not an account of a real happening,' and in saying this imagine that they have lessened the difficulty. But this is just not so. Christ does not indicate whether it is a parable or not, and this to my mind is not of great significance. I am personally inclined to take it as a parable, but immediately there rises the question: If this is figurative, what is the reality which it is depicting? It cannot be any less awful than the picture Christ uses to describe it.

What do we learn from the story? May I summarise a number of points?

There is life after death, and human identity endures.
Men are held accountable for their deeds on earth.
People divide into two groups and go into either Heaven or hell.
There is clear recognition of others in both places.
In Heaven and hell there is both knowledge and memory of the earth life.
Hell is a place of unutterable torment.
Between Heaven and hell there is a gulf fixed so that none may cross in either direction.
There is no hope in hell; it goes on for ever.

Let us look more closely at these points.

There is life after death, and human identity endures. It is very clear that Christ believed in and taught that there is an afterlife. His teaching here is consistent with His other sayings, for example, 'In my Father's house are many mansions; if it were not so, I would have told you; for I go to prepare a place for you' (Jn 14:2), and again, 'Whither I go, ye cannot come...except ye believe that I am he, ye shall die in your sins' (Jn 8:21,24). Human identity endures beyond the grave.

Men are held accountable for their deeds on earth. This clearly emerges from the story. There is a time of reckoning, and the condition in which a man dies affects his destiny beyond the grave. This is in line with Scripture generally. Judgment is clearly predicted. Men, we read, will give account of the deeds done in the body whether they are good or bad (cf. Rom 14:12; 2 Cor 5:10). John's picture of the great white throne is peculiarly apposite:

> And I saw a great white throne, and him that sat upon it, from whose face the earth and the heaven fled away; and there was found no place for them. And I saw the dead, the great and the small, standing before the throne; and books were opened: and another book was opened, which is the book of life: and the dead were judged out of the things which were written in the books, according to their works. And the sea gave up the dead which were in it; and death and Hades gave up the dead which were in them: and they were judged every man according to their works. And death and Hades were cast into the lake of fire. This is the second death, even the lake of fire. And if any was not found written in the book of life, he was cast into the lake of fire (Rev 20:11–15).

In particular, note the words, 'The dead were judged out of the things which were written in the books, according to their works.'

People divide into two groups and go into either Heaven or hell. There is no third or neutral position, and there is no annihilation. Many hope that at the end of life they will just cease to be, but neither here nor elsewhere in Scripture is there any suggestion of such happening. There is no middle way. I am reminded of John Oxenham's poem:

> To every man there openeth
> A Way, and Ways, and a Way.
> And the High Soul climbs the High Way,
> And the Low Soul gropes the Low,
> And in between, on the misty flats,
> The rest drift to and fro.
> But to every man there openeth
> A High Way, and a Low.
> And every man decideth
> The Way his soul shall go.

While there may seem to be three groups on earth, there are only two in eternity. There are no drifters on the misty flats.

There is clear recognition of others in both places. The rich man and Lazarus obviously recognised each other. Now this may not seem particularly remarkable, since they had known each other on earth. But what is remarkable is the fact that the rich man recognised Abraham whom he had never seen, just as Peter, James and John recognised Moses and Elijah on the Mount of Transfiguration without any introduction. 'We shall know,' as Paul wrote later of the eternal state, 'even as we are known.' This to most people is a mystery—but there are those who have had dealings in the inner spiritual world and have known with an absolute knowledge, which comes by spiritual revelation, that they are, for example, in the presence of Christ as distinct from an angel, or alternatively in the presence of an angel as distinct from Christ.[3] This does not come by mental cogitation. It is revealed as absolute truth. The normal thinking process is bypassed. Thus even on earth there are glimpses of what will be in eternity. We will need no introduction to Moses or David or Elijah. We will recognise with an absolute certainty, and we too will be wholly known.

In Heaven and hell there is both knowledge and memory of the earth life. Abraham's reference to the kind of lives that Lazarus and the rich man had lived revealed that he had knowledge of affairs that happened on earth long after his own lifetime. This is of great interest and raises the question of how much those who have gone on know of events on earth. The extent of it is not revealed, but that it *can* happen is clear. The writer to the Hebrews later wrote of our approach to the 'heavenly Jerusalem,' 'the city of the Living God,' to the 'church of the first born,' 'and to the spirits of just men made perfect' (Heb 12:22–23). He spoke too of being 'compassed about with...a cloud of witnesses.' The questions that rise from this are fascinating, but I should point out that Scripture gives us no warrant for trying to enter into communication with those who have gone on before. Warnings in the Old Testament against trying to contact the dead are dire, and the practice is totally forbidden. That does not mean that those who die in Christ have no knowledge of us, but whether they generally do, or the extent to which they do, or the reason for their knowing, is not revealed. We must leave it as mystery.

That there is memory of the earth life, with bitter regret, is clear. Lazarus and the rich man both recollected former days, and the rich man showed anxiety that his brothers be warned about hell lest they also share his fate. We should also note that Abraham actually said to the rich man, 'Son, remember....' These words, I always feel, are amongst the saddest and most sombre in Scripture. I remember one of the ablest preachers whom I ever heard, preach for about two and a half hours on these two words, and a dropping pin might have been heard in the silence of a spellbound audience. Yes, there is memory in hell, and memory for the lost will mean remorse, and remorse is a relentless agony.

> Memory's sea is deep and wide
>   And her waves are bitter cold.
> Memory's sea is cruel as death
>   And her waves remorseless roll.
> In their icy depths there gleams
>   The frustration of the soul.

'Son, remember.' The rich man was still a son of Abraham, but he was a lost son.

Hell is a place of unutterable torment. We come to the core of the agony: 'Send Lazarus, that he may dip the tip of his finger in water, and cool my tongue; for I am in anguish in this flame.' We must neither add to this, nor take from it. I am utterly convinced of its truth. Through the ages many a soul has had overpowering revelation of hell—sometimes in vision or in dream or through inescapable conviction. In revival times the experience is widespread. Those who have it never forget and are never the same again. I remember the effect which the tract 'A Year and a Day' had on me in my own early days. In the nineteenth century Francis Dashwood, a young nobleman who was president of the Hell Fire Club, had a remarkable dream. He was living a dissolute and godless life and presided over a society which was bent on evil. In his dream he found himself in hell with all its horror. As he was guided from place to place he particularly noticed a constant movement—indeed frenetic activity. On questioning his guide he was told, 'There is no rest in hell.' (This conforms remarkably to the experience of one of my own friends who also had a vision of hell. In her case she saw many roads converging on a centre and people were endlessly hurrying in all directions—forever seeking and never finding what they sought. There was no fulfilment and never rest.) Before his visit ended he was warned that in a year and a day he would be back in hell. He wakened on earth profoundly shocked and for a time made some effort to amend his ways and acquaint himself with the Bible. He was, however, ashamed to be found reading it and when the annual meeting of the club came round—always a year and a day after the previous meeting—he made the critical decision to go. There had been a time of vacillating when hope at least still burned, but now the die was cast. He went, and in the morning a riderless horse made its way home. He lay dead by the roadway. It was exactly a year and a day after his revelation of hell. That too had come on the evening of a meeting of the Hell Fire Club.[4]

It is not unusual for evangelists to have revelation of hell and it is for their great good. Indeed, General Booth, the founder of the Salvation Army, would have liked all his preachers to have been shaken over hell for at least a brief period. I understand him. Those who have the experience do not develop as lightweight preachers or entertainers of the people. They are deeply serious and realise their true vocation. They preach as dying men to dying men and the cry of the lost is in their ears. The great issues of eternity are graven on their hearts. May I emphasize that life to those who have this experience is never the same again.

I speak with personal knowledge. Once in my youth I was in danger of taking a wrong way and I had a dream—different from any ordinary dream I ever had. In it I was being carried or helping to carry another into a flaming hell. The horror was indescribable. I cannot put it into words. It doesn't exist in the realm of the mind—it is a felt horror—an atmosphere indescribable in normal ways. Totally different from earth life. For me too life was never the same again. The knowledge of a depth of horror and endless pain was indelibly imprinted on my being—a horror beyond imagining. Flames that live forever in my memory.

Between Heaven and hell there is a gulf fixed so that none may cross in either direction. After indicating the way in which the rich man had lived and the consequences, Abraham went on to use the words which sound like a knell: 'And beside all this, between us and you there is a great gulf fixed, that they which would pass from hence to you may not be able, and that none may cross over from thence to us.' To me, the awful words here are not so much 'a great gulf' but the one word 'fixed.' The divide was great, but that might be tolerable. There might be a way over. But the further words extinguish hope: 'they which would pass from hence to you may not be able, and...none may cross over from thence to us.' There is no way over, and as though that was not enough we are told that the gulf is 'fixed.' It is not a temporary divide—it is fixed—fixed for all eternity. Again I instinctively feel—ring down the curtain. We cannot bear to look further in. It is an intolerable agony.[5]

There is no hope in hell; it goes on for ever. There is no cessation of pain and no gleam of light for some future time. Surely one of the most awful things about hell is its hopelessness. (I am finding a most peculiar thing in writing this chapter. It is far and away the most difficult I have tried to write. I feel myself deeply opposed. Satan himself is opposing me. I feel as though God gives illumination and I have the awful experience of having thoughts snatched out of my mind before I get them down. The truth about hell and judgment Satan hates to have revealed to men—but greater is He that is for us than all that can come against us. Glory to God, and by His grace the chapter will be fully written.) It is this conception of a torment going on for ever and ever and ever that breaks so many a mind. We are not really equipped to deal with the concept of infinity, either in space or in time. The mind staggers before it. Our minds are finite and may deal with finite things. They were never created to compass eternity. It is as though a man tried to cross the Atlantic on a bicycle. It just can't be done. Bicycles were never built for that purpose. Perhaps when we ourselves are in eternity we will begin to understand the infinite. Here on earth we see but the edges of His ways, and the lifting of the curtain showing but the edges of hell is more than we can easily bear.

It is little wonder that good men have sought alternative explanations. Some have preached the reality of hell—but put forward a case for ultimate reconciliation at some future point, as for example in 'the ages of the ages.' Many would like to think so, but it seems to me that the balance of Scripture does not support the view. What the work of Christ did not achieve in rescuing a soul on earth, the sufferings of hell will never do. The whole tenor of John's writings in Revelation is against it. There death and hell are seen cast into the lake of fire—the eternal abode of Satan and his angels. Here there are eternal burnings.

> And the devil that deceived them was cast into the lake of fire and brimstone, where are also the beast and the false prophet; and they shall be tormented day and night for ever and ever.... And death and Hades were cast into the lake of fire. This is the second death, even the lake of fire (Rev 20:10,14).

The words are very grave and no special pleading can evade their import.

There is another part of the teachings of Christ which concerns the same subject. We read in Mark's Gospel:

> And if thy hand cause thee to stumble, cut it off: it is good for thee to enter into life maimed, rather than having thy two hands to go into hell, into the unquenchable fire. And if thy foot cause thee to stumble, cut it off: it is good for thee to enter into life halt, rather than having thy two feet to be cast into hell. And if thine eye cause thee to stumble, cast it out: it is good for thee to enter into the kingdom of God with one eye, rather than having two eyes to be cast into hell; where their worm dieth not, and the fire is not quenched (Mk 9:43–48).

In brief, this corroborates the story of the rich man in Luke's writings and speaks of endless suffering for the soul who goes to hell.[6] If the hand (speaking of the thing one does) offends, it is better to be cut off than be the means of taking the whole man to hell. Similarly with the foot (speaking of the places one goes) or the eye (denoting the things one sees). In short, if anything is preventing a man taking the right way—any rebellious part of his body or being—he is well advised to cut it out ruthlessly rather than suffer the loss of his whole being. This is straightforward gospel teaching and is a note that should be clearly sounded.

Finally, my reader friend (if you are still my friend), I advise you to take life as it is and not necessarily as you might like it to be. Become a realist. Your revulsion at the idea of hell has no bearing on whether it exists or does not. Truth for ever stands and is unaffected by our conception of it. To my mind, and this may surprise you, the doctrine of hell is one of the easiest of all Christian doctrines to prove. Show me a man who is already in the grip of deep sin and I will show you a man in whose eyes the fires of hell already burn. Have you ever seen the desperate drug addict who has struggled and failed to find freedom, the alcoholic who hates his addiction but cannot break it, the demon-possessed in whose eyes hell smoulders? Yes, on earth there is the beginning of hell. Let any man go the way of evil and let evil develop, and he will begin to feel the pains of hell—yes, even in this life. You see, hell is not a geographic location, somewhere at the centre of earth or on some further star. It is a spiritual location related to another dimension—but its spiritual effects are felt on earth, in time, although its fulfilment will be in eternity.

Now the horror of the sin-ridden is observable on earth, in this life, amongst people we know. These are facts: let us deal with facts. Also, the problem of pain is one of the most difficult we have to face, and while I do not want to go down that line in detail here, we must recognise that pain exists. It may seem terribly unfair—but a little toddler, for example, may fall against an electric fire and be burned. The child may linger in agony for weeks and then die, or recover and be handicapped for life. To many a mind this is quite intolerable—but intolerable or no, it is a fact. It happens. Life is like this. If there can be such pain as there observably is on earth, why does its existence in the next life seem impossible? The human spirit is capable of incredible pain and suffering on earth. Why should it be supposed that this will alter by the process of dying? Surely these are rather pointers to what lies beyond the grave. We are capable of righteousness and wonderful joy, of desperate evil and pain beyond expression. There is no reason to believe that these states will not continue and indeed intensify in the beyond.

Many a question floods to the mind. What about the heathen who never hear the gospel? What about children who die before they reach an age of responsibility? In my view no man ever enters the kingdom of Heaven other than through the work of Christ. Old Testament saints lived before His day and their sacrifices pointed to His own. They were justified not by works but were accepted on the ground of the work of One who was to come. Their sacrifices were not acceptable unless they had a right attitude to God and to their sin. They lived before Christ's day, we after it, but the positions are very similar. We are not saved on the ground of our good works but on the ground of His perfect work—but if we regard iniquity in our hearts God does not hear us. If our attitude is not right, if we are not truly repentant, we are not received. *They* looked forward to the Cross; *we* look backward; but neither they nor we are justified on the ground of works. Salvation is the provision of God.

Thus the Old Testament saints were saved through blood that was not yet shed. Where the unevangelised heathen are concerned, I believe the truth of 'consciences excusing or accusing' is relevant. There are amongst them those who have tried to live right according to their lights and consciences. I believe they are few but that for them the blood of Christ will avail. For the vast majority it is otherwise. Unless the wonderful miracle that the gospel works takes place in their darkened hearts, they will inevitably be lost.

Similarly, I believe the blood of Christ avails for children who die before reaching an age of responsibility.

Finally, let me say that I never conceive of God sending anybody to hell. Men go to hell in spite of God. God created man, made man perfect and provided for his earth life. He sinned and came under the domain of Satan, whom he had chosen to serve rather than God. God made a way of salvation. This he opened to all men and at tremendous cost to Himself. He gave His only beloved Son to provide a ransom. The Son gave Himself—gave His very life for man. To all, the invitation is given to come and receive life and forgiveness. Those who come receive it. None who comes is ever turned away. None is ever received who does not come. God has made adequate provision. He has given full encouragement. He has given fearful warning of the consequences of refusing His salvation. How can any man blame God for the loss of a soul or hold God responsible for sending men to hell? Surely He has revealed Himself as being in the business of saving men from hell and that at awful cost. Satan it is who is responsible for the fate of the lost. We chose him in our first forefather—we are born in his domain and hell is the inevitable consequence of the condition, if this does not alter. God moves to alter it and a choice is put before us—we can choose good or evil, God or Satan. If we choose wrongly we sin against clear light. We destine ourselves to hell. We cannot blame God. He has done nothing but good and shown an endless mercy. If, against that goodness, that mercy, that sacrifice, we stubbornly refuse His salvation, we must accept the blame.

Could I direct your gaze again to Calvary? In the light of that suffering, that sacrifice, who can possibly say that God has not done all He could do to save the souls of men and stop the road to hell? No, friend, if you go there, your fate will be entirely, or perhaps I should say, with the aid of the devil, of your own making.

I have deliberately refrained from undue philosophising or vain speculation in this chapter. I have kept the matter straightforward and scripturally accurate. There is, however, one further point I would like to emphasise. In times of revival the doctrines of hell and judgment come to the fore again and again. Amongst the functions of the Holy Spirit mentioned by Christ are the bringing of conviction of sin, righteousness and judgment. It is ever so. I remember hearing from the late Rev Duncan Campbell of Lewis revival fame that such had been his message in the country parts of Lewis where revival had run like fire. The time came when he was due to preach in Stornoway and he wondered if he should alter his message for the more sophisticated and southernised capital. God forbade it. The message was exactly the same—and if and when revival comes these disturbing truths will surge again to the surface. In times of declension Satan sees to it that they are buried deep. It is fashionable to pour contempt on the doctrine of hell. It is very perturbing, very disturbing, indeed to many, repulsive—totally objectionable. Even in some evangelical circles Mr Campbell's emphasis on the doctrine was not happily received, and in today's world it is scarcely likely to be any more popular.

These facts I gleaned from Mr Campbell. There is another I heard about him, and I have reason to believe it is true. Prior to the outbreak of revival, before going out in the work that led to it, he had a vision of the young people of the Hebrides going into hell. He was profoundly affected and the consequences were glorious as revival visited the islands. He felt the burning of hell and transmitted the horror of it. How shall we transmit fire if we have never known the heart of the fire?

I will close with a wonderful story of one old Highland lady. She knew her Bible, she understood and believed in the doctrine of hell—but there came an hour when she heard hell preached under the power of the Holy Spirit. It became intensely alive and real to her and she exclaimed, 'The hell of the Bible is terrible—but oh, the hell of Duncan Campbell!' Would to God that this awareness would come upon the Church. Then would souls be saved and saved in depth. As they say in the Highlands, they would be well born. Few such ever backslide.

For further light on this whole subject read, for example, Charles Finney, Jonathan Edwards,[7] certain visions of Marietta Davies,[8] and the more recent work of C. S. Lewis.[9]

Notes

[1] Hades, as it was known in Christ's day.

[2] A way of referring to the abode of the blest.

[3] I know about this from personal experience as well as from study. The sense of absolute knowledge which comes with such experiences quite apart from normal mental processes, is quite remarkable. It has happened to me at different times in life, generally at points of crisis and strangely enough often in some way connected with the Island of Lewis. There I have known the ministry of angels—although I don't want to open up this theme here.

[4] I understand the caves in which the club met may still be visited at High Wycombe.

[5] There is a sense in which we tend to think in almost physical terms in considering hell. We should endeavour to see beyond this to the spiritual dimension. Perhaps the real *heart of hell* lies in the fact that man was made for God and can never be fulfilled outside of God, and with the 'fixed gulf' all hope dies of this ever happening. The final parting from the source of life is unutterable hell. No hope for evermore. It is worse than, at a

physical level, having a limb torn from the body. It is final alienation.

[6] The question rises: how can there be a burning which does not consume? We should understand that our bodies in the afterlife will be fitted to their environment—whether Heaven or hell. They will not be earth bodies, and as bricks in a brick kiln are themselves salted by fire and do not perish in the burning—so the bodies of the lost will burn but endure the burning.

[7] Particularly his sermon on 'Sinners in the Hands of an Angry God.'

[8] Gordon Lindsay, ed., *Scenes Beyond the Grave: Visions of Marietta Davis* (The Voice of Healing Publishing Co., n.d.). Purported visions of Heaven and hell must of course be treated with great care. Even so, there is much food for thought in the visions of hell portrayed in this book.

[9] In chap. 4 of *The Problem of Pain* (Collins, Fount Paperbacks, 1980), C. S. Lewis approaches the subject of hell in quite a different way. He attempts a moral/philosophical justification of the doctrine. In his own words, '...let us make no mistake; it is not tolerable. But I think the doctrine can be shown to be moral, by a critique of the objections ordinarily made, or felt, against it...' (p. 108). Readers may find that this approach is complementary to my own writing, which tends to be biblically and experientially based. Lewis' work contains some salutory truths—as when, for example, he writes that Christ's 'utterances about Hell, like all [His] sayings, are addressed to the conscience and the will, not to our intellectual curiosity...' (p. 107).

10

Meet my Friend or *Precisely What Must I Do to Be Saved?*

There are some preachers who, after addressing their audiences on subjects such as salvation, healing, exorcism, baptism in the Spirit, bring their services quickly to a close. There are others who at the end of preaching say, 'That is the theory: shall we now pass from theory to practice?' They open themselves and encourage others to be open to the action of God so that what has been taught may be outworked. They believe in the action of God in the 'now,' and again and again God honours this. Shall we regard much of the foregoing writing as the theory (in one limited sense of that word), which it may ever remain to the reader who does not act on it, and pass to the realm of practice?

I address the reader who, while interested in Christianity, has never made a full commitment to Christ, who in the old-fashioned but still appropriate language, has never been saved and who would like to know how precisely to be saved.

'Precisely what must I do to be saved?'[1]

This to some may seem a ridiculously simple question. I find, however, that when I ask Christians in groups or individually to answer the question it does not seem simple at all and surprisingly few have taken time to think the matter through and find satisfactory answers. Too often the replies are vague and general and of little help to enquirers. Now perhaps I have certain advantages over some others, in that I have been a teacher. A teacher does not necessarily know more than many others do, but normally he does know more about how little people learn from vague instructions, and he learns to break down his lessons into easily absorbed parts. Bruner, the educational philosopher, taught that more or less everybody could be taught most things if these were broken down small enough. That may or may not be true, but it is certainly true that vague general teaching is normally unproductive.

In the educational field we live in an age of closely defined aims and objectives—short and long term goals. A lesson is seen as a means whereby cognitive change will be effected in the pupils who receive it. They are expected to be different at the end of it. The teacher is expected to know precisely where he is going. Knowledge is to be handled in a way which will make it easily assimilated. In the secular sphere these matters are seriously approached. In the spiritual world we should be no less particular.

Do not regard the foregoing as unnecessarily fussy or merely some modern fad. I remember that in my earliest days I taught enthusiastically. I worked very hard. All my pupils were going to perform brilliantly. I set the first examinations and discovered that while I had been working strenuously, they had been working not at all. My words of wisdom had winged their way right over their unheeding heads. They had looked intelligent and been thinking—of other things. I had talked on and they had let me talk. They performed disgracefully and I had some serious thinking to do. First I decided that where they had relaxed and I had worked, I would now relax a little and they would work! I went back to first principles. I remembered my psychology lectures where the process of learning was examined in detail. I remember to this day the example of how a biology lesson could be approached. It went as follows:

Teacher:	*Statement.*	A plant has two parts.
	Question.	How many parts has a plant?
Pupil:	*Answer.*	Two.
Teacher:	*Statement.*	The two parts are a root and a shoot.
	Question.	What are the two parts?
Pupil:	*Answer.*	A root and a shoot.

Quite ridiculous! you exclaim. Far too simple and indeed childish! Not so, my friend, not so. I went into my first class after my reassessment of things and put this into operation in a history lesson. Proceedings went something like this. First I spoke quietly so that badly-behaved pupils who were making a noise would not hear me and thereby give me ground for dealing with them. My dealings produced a welcome silence. I then repeated the unheard statement with the appropriate question:

Teacher:	*Statement.*	King William of Normandy defeated King Harold of England at the Battle of Hastings.
	Question.	Who defeated King Harold at the Battle of Hastings?
Selected Pupil:		(Silence)
Teacher:		Come out here (these were the days of corporal punishment in Scottish schools—a moderate palmy—not enough to hurt too much but enough to focus attention!).
Teacher:	*Statement.*	King William of Normandy defeated King Harold of England at the Battle of Hastings.

Question. Who defeated King Harold at the Battle of Hastings?
(Every hand in the class goes up.)
Selected Pupil: King William, sir.

I had their attention. I kept it. I proceeded step by step and they learned. Oh yes, they learned and from that day on performance greatly improved. I too had learned my lesson—no longer high-falutin' theories about kingship and vague feudal notions, but knowledge appropriate to the ages of my charges and their ability to absorb it. Nothing vague and woolly either in the substance of the lesson or in its presentation. It works.

Now should we be any less particular in the spiritual realm, especially in the vitally important matter of the salvation of the soul? Surely not! So how shall we approach it?

First, perhaps I should explain one or two significant background points which can be very important to enquirers.

No man can save himself, nor be saved simply because he decides to make a commitment. True salvation always involves the 'new birth' and comes not by the will of man but by the operation of the Holy Spirit. Christ made this very clear to Nicodemus in John 3. 'Ye must,' He said, 'be born again.' It was a divine imperative. 'The wind bloweth where it listeth, and thou hearest the voice thereof, but knowest not whence it cometh, and whither it goeth: so is every one that is born of the Spirit.' Thus while we are dependent on the action of God we are also responsible to respond to His movement, His word.

Now we can be entirely confident that God will play His part perfectly. We can depend on Him altogether and we learn from Scripture that: 'God so loved the world, that he gave his only begotten Son, that whosoever believeth on him should not perish, but have eternal life' (John 3:16). In other words, the love of God reaches out to men. He is more anxious to save them than they are to be saved. He sent His Son to die for precisely this purpose. Christ gave His life willingly for this very thing: therefore we can be assured of God's attitude to a repentant sinner. 'God willeth not that any should perish but that all should come to a knowledge of the truth.' It makes such a difference to a person to know how another will receive him if there has been a serious barrier between them and he is returning to put matters right. Sometimes a breach occurs between friends and a hardness has developed over the years. One longs for reconciliation but sadly fears that any advance he makes will be repulsed: he hears through a third party that his estranged friend longs to see him again. Knowing this attitude makes it so much easier for him to approach the other. To make God's attitude clearly known Christ one day told three parables dealing with a lost son ('the prodigal son'), a lost sheep and a lost coin. He showed the tremendous joy there was in each case when that which was lost was found. 'So,' He said, 'there shall be joy in heaven over one sinner that repenteth.'

This gives you great encouragement to come—but before you come I would draw your attention to one word in the last sentence: 'repenteth.' The first word John the Baptist ever preached was, 'Repent,' and most Bible readers know this. What many do not know is that the same word is the first that is recorded in Christ's preaching. I must emphasise the importance of repentance. There is no place in the Bible for a cheap 'believism' and this is too frequently taught in some circles. 'Just raise your hand for Christ. Just fill your name into John 3:16 and you will be saved.' No word of sin, or repentance of sin. It can lead to pseudo-conversion and tragedy. People will come back and say, 'I was saved but it hasn't made any difference to me.' The truth is they were never saved; no change has taken place in their lives. I remember hearing Duncan Campbell using awful words in this connection. He referred to John 3:16 and said he feared that that verse would be responsible for sending more people to hell than he cared to imagine. He did not mean, of course, that the verse would be responsible, but that preachers' wrong interpretation of it and people's wrong understanding of it would.[2] A 'believism' that involves no repentance for sin can be very dangerous. Always remember that when the Bible speaks of believing on Christ for salvation, the belief was related to the Messiahship of Christ—to his being the Son of God as He had declared Himself to be. For an Israelite to recognise this meant automatic submission and following. It brought him into a relationship with not only a Saviour but a Lord. For non-Jews things are different—there may be mental acquiescence with the idea that Jesus was the Son of God without the slightest commitment to have Him rule the life. There can be a believism that involves no lordship and results in no conversion. There *is* a contract and involved in it is the taking of Christ as Lord and Master. Never be mistaken on this point.

In my own case I sought Christ for years without finding Him. Many counsellors tried to help, but to no avail, until one of them asked me pointedly if there was any sin in my life. The connection between sin and salvation had never come home to me sharply before. There *was* sin. For years I had been desperate for salvation—but never found it. Now I began to understand, and I remember making the moral decision that from that hour I would live as I believed a Christian should live whether God received me or not. I would wait, if need be, at Heaven's door for the rest of a lifetime. Within about an hour of the moral decision, light broke and I found Christ and had assurance of salvation.

Finally, on the theme of repentance, let me speak of my observations of Billy Graham campaigns in Scotland. At the time of Billy's visits there were many gospel preachers in Britain, but comparatively few seemed to be greatly used in winning souls. I observed one great difference between Billy and many others. In his preaching he emphasised sin. He brought it sharply to the fore and masses of people were affected. I noticed that on nights when a broken commandment was the theme of his address a brooding hush filled the hall and the response was particularly great. Emphasis on sin and the broken law of God brought conviction and repentance, and repentance led to a cry for mercy—to which cry God was never deaf. Many passed from death to life. I counselled many at these gatherings and this may seem a sad and serious thing to say—but the majority of those I counselled were already fully-communicating members of churches and they discovered under anointed preaching that they had never been truly saved. Yes, they had heard about Billy. He seemed such a handsome American and it was good that people should be encouraged into the churches; it was not, of course, for them but they would like to hear him. They went and he began to preach. This would do their neighbours good. Suddenly he is not speaking to their neighbours, he is addressing them. Suddenly it is not Billy who is addressing them; it is God, Himself. The audience vanishes, Billy vanishes and they are alone with an offended God—offended but seeking to bring them to a place of repentance and reconciliation. Christ is presented, the one and only way of salvation, and they are wonderfully relieved to accept His terms. There, having secured seats at the furthest parts of the hall, they have to walk the long way down. There from the choir they come. There it was known for even a counsellor to take his badge from his lapel and throw it on the floor and stand with the penitent at the front of the stage. People who thought they belonged to Christ suddenly realised that while they belonged to the church they had never had a personal encounter with Jesus and they realised, as did Nicodemus of old, that they had to be 'born again.' There is no other way than this. We are not born into Christianity by natural birth; we don't grow into it automatically. Being born in a Christian home or joining a Christian church does not effect the change. It is like marriage. It is something which involves a personal encounter, a personal commitment. It never happens by chance. No soul drifts into it.

There is another very relevant matter. On what basis does God save a soul? What provision has been made for the cancellation of the debt of sin? We read: 'All we like sheep have gone astray; we have turned everyone to his own way; and the Lord hath laid on him the iniquity of us all' (Isaiah 53:6). The fact is that human sin was laid on Christ. He died for it. His blood made a full atonement and God can now be both just and the justifier of all who come unto Him by Christ. This may seem a difficult conception and the question may rise: how could one life atone for the untold millions of mankind? The fact is that every human life is finite and any number of finite lives do not make up the sum of one infinite life. The life of Christ was an infinite life—a perfect life and an adequate atonement for humanity. That His sacrifice was acceptable to God is evidenced by the fact that God raised Him from the dead. The truth may be very simply stated but it is profound. The truth is that there was facing each of us a debt no man could ever pay. He paid it all by His one sacrifice for sin forever and offers full pardon to all who come to Him at Calvary. It is like a person having a friend who pays an outstanding debt. The creditor cannot again require payment. As the hymn puts it:

He will not payment twice demand,
First at my bleeding Surety's hand
And then again at mine.

Or, to vary the metaphor, a person could be in prison and an amnesty is declared: all he has to do to obtain freedom is sign himself out, but he must come and ask for that pardon. So with Christ: the pardon is offered at Calvary, but every man must come for it individually. None who comes is turned away and none is ever received who does not come.

Yes, a full and adequate provision for our salvation has been made by Christ. He has carried our sins. He has made atonement for our souls. He died in our place and by His blood we are cleansed. Make no mistake, Christ did not live on earth merely to set us a good example, to show us how men ought to live. He came to die. The man born to be king was born to die on the Cross. His death was substitutionary. He died in our place. Thus in our approach to God we can have perfect confidence that the way of salvation has been fully secured for us, secured by Christ, secured by blood.

Having established at least some of the background, let us come to precise steps to salvation itself. You know of the need for the new birth. You know of God's love and attitude to all men. You know of the provision He has made for you at Calvary. You know of the need for true repentance and I can hear you say, 'Yes, I know all of these things, but what now in practical terms must I actually do?'

I want you to picture Christ present and hear Him saying to you personally what He has said to all men generally, 'Come unto me all ye that labour and are heavy laden, and I will give you rest,' and again, 'He that cometh unto me I will in no wise cast out.' There you have an offer and the offer comes from the Son of God. Now an offer forms the basis of a contract and a contract is something into which the party making the offer and the party accepting it both enter. The very fact of an offer implies the possibility of its acceptance. Thus the onus immediately comes upon the enquirer. The offer is there in the words of Christ. What, if any, are the conditions? There are two which are immediately apparent. First, action is demanded. The person must come. None who comes is ever rejected. None is ever received who does not come. To come means to come to a Person; it implies commitment to Him, becoming His. He does not promise life or rest apart from Himself. These things are found in Himself. The soul becomes wedded to Him. It becomes His. Secondly, to come to Him implies coming away from something else—it involves turning the back on a life of sin and self-pleasing, of being one's own person, or being under Satan's rule. This is the meaning of conversion. It means a turning right round about. 'Except ye turn, and become as little children, ye shall in no wise enter into the kingdom of heaven.' No man 'regarding iniquity in his heart' may hope to be received. There must be a new attitude, an intention to go God's way—to serve Him, to turn completely from all wrong ways, to be truly repentant, which really means that a state of mind and attitude is reached where, had you life to live over again, you would act differently in respect to wrongdoing, in so far as you were able. This is true repentance. It is more than mere sorrow for sin. It implies a new attitude to it, past and present and future.

Thus we have the basis of a contract. Christ is there; His offer is there; the conditions are there and you are there. What must you now do? At this point I normally illustrate from a normal wedding situation the need to make the contract definite. A young man and woman are in love. They approach me to marry them. Arrangements are made. The day arrives. The groom and best man are before me awaiting the coming of the bride and her bridesmaids. At last they come up the aisle. Now at this point, while they love each other, they are not married. If by some fearful chance one or other at that moment takes a heart attack and dies, they will remain unmarried. They undoubtedly loved each other. They had every intention of marrying but the contract has not been made. They remain unmarried. In normal circumstances there comes the moment when I formally say, 'Do you, John, take Jean, the woman you now hold by the right hand, to be your lawful wedded wife?' to which he replies, 'I do,' and I then reverse the question to Jean, who similarly replies. I then pronounce them lawfully wedded husband and wife. They have entered into a contract, witnessed by others, which is legally binding. They are married.

Now in a spiritual marriage, which a salvation really is, I say to the person, 'I have been authorised by Christ to preach the gospel and offer men salvation on His terms. I am merely the instrument and I want you now to forget me and hear His voice directly. He says, 'Come.' What is your response?' Again and again it is, 'Yes, I come.' I then say, 'Do you believe He has received you?' Often there is a pause and I become aware of doubt. I then say, 'Look, friend, here is my Bible. Were I to say, 'Put out your hand and it will be yours,' you would know that if I am a man of my word and you put out your hand it would be yours. Now on what is such trust based?' If the person knows me really well he will have no doubt at all. He would trust, not simply on the basis of what I said, but on the basis of my character and integrity. So it is with Christ. He has given His solemn word to receive all who come. I then put this simply to the enquirer: 'You would believe me if I promised you my Bible.'—'Yes.' 'You would believe me not just because of what I said but because of your trust in me as a person.'—'Yes.' 'Now if you can trust me, a fallible man, how much more can you trust Christ, the sinless Son of God?' This is not difficult for the enquirer to appreciate. 'Then do you believe He was the kind of person who was totally trustworthy?'—'Yes.' 'That everything He said was true, that every promise He made He would keep?'—'Yes.' 'Do you believe His word? Do you believe He has given you salvation? You would have believed me over the offer of the Bible. Do you believe Him? You can base your faith on His character and His word.'—'Yes, I do. I see it now.' That is faith and at that point the soul may pass from death into life. The contract is now sealed as in a marriage. I have no need to assure the couple of what has happened. It shines on their faces. They know they are married. So when souls go genuinely through the stages I have outlined, again and again I have no need to say, 'Now you are saved.' It shines on their faces.

The next day dawns and an enquirer comes back to say that he felt good last night but he does not feel so good today. Is he still saved? 'Friend,' I say, 'are you married?' If the answer is yes, I continue, 'On the morning you first wakened after marriage, did it matter how you felt? You had entered into a contract that did not depend on your *feelings*. Whether you felt married or did not, the fact remained that you *were* married. Similarly, your relationship with Christ depends on *His word*, not on *your feelings*. Your new birth came by an operation of the Holy Spirit and does not depend for its validity on your later feelings either about it, or about your own condition. Feelings may change from day to day; His word, never to all eternity. This gives stable ground for the soul's total confidence. Not only does God save our souls, but He gives us assurance of salvation.

God's servant can depend on God to make the way of salvation plain to the truly seeking soul. If, however, an insincere person comes and indeed goes through all the motions, no true conversion will result. We are forever dependent on the action of the Holy Spirit to effect the new birth.

This is as simple as I can make this matter—simple enough, I trust, for any seeking souls to go on their knees before God and find Him in Christ Jesus our Lord. Do meet my Friend. May God bless you.

★ ★ ★

And so we come to an end. I would leave with you four of our questions—amongst the most important questions human ears ever hear or human minds consider:

What think ye of Christ?
What shall I do with Jesus Who is called Christ?
What shall it profit a man if he gains the whole world and loses his own soul?
What must I do to be saved?

Notes

[1] The Bible teaches that man is lost to God as a result of sin. Through Christ he can be saved from both the power and the penalty of sin. The Philippian jailer asked Paul the question, 'What must I do to be saved?' and received the answer, 'Believe on the Lord Jesus Christ...and thou shalt be saved.' The terms 'saved,' 'changed,' 'converted,' 'born again' are frequently used by Christian writers to describe the same experience. Our redemption was obtained at Calvary, and in the moment of coming to Christ a soul is born again. But the full consequences of salvation will not be experienced until the hereafter.

[2] Readers may notice that I have frequently referred to Mr Campbell. This is simply because he preached much that I found very valuable, but I feel I should also make it clear that on certain issues we did not agree.

PART 2

At the Mouth of Two Witnesses

Introducing Susie and Pauline

As has been my practice in recent books, I am again including testimony—this time the stories of two young ladies, twins, who came to Christ about ten years ago and have been wonderfully changed. Susie is now married and her husband Paul holds a weekly house meeting in which she is involved. She has an unusual ministry of intercession. Time and again, clear revelation of the needs of others and of spiritual situations generally is given. Satan's strategy is discerned and with revelation comes burden of prayer. Revelation is a very real thing and is wholly accurate in its operation. I can myself testify to the value of this ministry from personal experience; in a time of very real need God gave Susie revelation about a situation in which I was deeply concerned. Her knowledge was absolutely accurate. A burden of prayer accompanied this and I deeply appreciated her ministry.

Over the last six months Susie has also been used in deliverance ministry, and not only has she power in prayer in this realm, but she also actually sees what is happening when a person is being set free. This is extremely valuable.

Finally, she has an insatiable appetite for the salvation of others. It is a constant driving force in her life and she has proved to be a faithful witness. Her life conforms to the story she tells.

Pauline followed Susie into the world six minutes later and into the kingdom about a month after her sister. She has shown a most unusual single-mindedness in her spiritual life. From the moment she became wholly committed to Christ she has set herself very high standards. By nature a very private person and more reserved than her sister, Pauline is being deeply used of God.

She is in charge of a house group where her preaching ministry is steadily developing. She is studiously inclined and is involved in the book side of my own ministry.

A short time after her conversion Pauline had a remarkable experience of liberation which has had a critical effect on her life. She became aware at that time of the absolute strength of Christ and within the last nine months she has known that same iron power entering her in a special way. God has taken her into a new dimension and immediately He began to use her in deliverance—in scores of cases over recent months. This ministry is very real and very valuable. In one of the first cases in which she was involved, I remember the young minister who was prayed for asked me later to let her know that as her hands were laid on him heat passed through his body. He was wonderfully helped. The power of this ministry is increasing and Pauline shows both strength and sensitivity in dealing with those in need. The call of God is upon her.

She too has an insatiable appetite for the salvation of others and the deliverance of those in deepest need. She shows particular concern for the lives God has put in her care. She has a pioneering spirit and is prepared to go to new places and break new ground, recently being involved in the Hebrides. Finally, her life testifies to the reality of her own experience of God. The fire of God burns in her. She is a faithful servant.

At the time of writing, Susie and Pauline with their sister Linda are attending to their widowed mother, who is terminally ill.* Theirs is a close-knit family, and I have noticed that they show a devotion to duty and a depth of care that is consistent with their Christian profession. Not only in theory, but in practical things, their religion is, as the Americans might say, 'for real.'

In earlier books I have used the testimonies of Christians who have been longer on the road than these two young ladies. But in this, my first gospel book, it may be that youth will be more ready to listen to their own generation than to mine. I trust that their experiences will encourage others to find the Saviour Who has so wonderfully transformed their lives.

*Mrs Anderson has since passed away.

SUSIE

11

First Encounter

From as far back as I can remember, I went to church every Sunday. I could have counted on one hand the number of times I missed over the years. I went week in, week out, year in, year out. I was brought up in the Catholic Church, and every Sunday morning we went as a family to nine o'clock mass, and this was the pattern of things until I was seventeen years old. Every Sunday, the priest spoke of us as being Christians and I never for one moment thought that perhaps I wasn't a Christian, perhaps there was something that I myself had to do about becoming one. Deep down I really did believe that because I was a Catholic, that automatically rubber-stamped me 'Christian,' and as I was never challenged along these lines, it never crossed my mind that this wasn't the case.

Life went by fairly uneventfully. There were no amazing peaks or troughs. Materially, I didn't want for anything, and there was no reason why I shouldn't have been totally happy. In due time I left school and went to college, where I studied catering and hotel management. As you enter the college and university scene, you feel that life is really going to open up for you. There are the pubs and the dances, just the normal teenage scene, and I was no different from all the others. My college was in the centre of Glasgow and so at lunchtime we all went to the pub, and in the evening there was the pub again and dancing. But at a time when life was supposed to be opening up for me, I found a real depression began to set in; and it wasn't just a general 'fed-upness' with life: I felt that no matter what I did, things would never change. There were times when I really tried to do something about it, but it just never worked.

Things went on like this for quite some time and I eventually decided that if I went away far enough and for long enough, things would be different when I came back. If I went to a place where nobody knew me and started afresh, then perhaps things would alter. I went to the Island of Skye, and the people whom I was working for called themselves Christians. I thought, 'Well, they're Protestant and I'm Catholic: that will be the difference.' But as I watched their lives, I realised there was something far more than any formal difference between Catholics and Protestants. To these people, Jesus Christ was a real and living Person, and I realised that the difference between their Christianity and my Christianity was that I knew *about* God, but they actually knew *Him*. Yes, I could have told you that Jesus Christ was born in Bethlehem about 2,000 years ago, that He was brought up in Nazareth and died on a cross and rose from the dead and went back to Heaven; I knew all these things, as did those Skye Christians. But my knowledge of Jesus was a head knowledge and theirs was from the heart. My first reaction was to have absolutely nothing to do with this Christianity, and in fact I was very scathing about these Christians. They used to get down on their knees as a family and pray together and I could not cope with this at all. Families just did not kneel together and pray in the twentieth century as far as I was concerned. I used to go and tell other people what these strange folk did, and their behaviour was put in the category of 'weird.' I remember writing home and telling my family about these 'weird' goings on; I very glibly said, 'Huh—God—that's all I need,' when in actual fact I should have realised then and there that yes, truly, God *was* all I needed, but it didn't register with me at all.

I had been a few months on the island when one day I walked in and noticed a book lying on a table. My boss told me to take it and read it. The book, called *Joni*, had just come out in this country and told the story of a girl who at seventeen years of age had broken her neck in a diving accident and been paralysed from the shoulders down. It told of how she came to trust God. As I read the book there came again through the pages the same thing I had heard while working at the hotel: that Jesus Christ is real and is alive today.

I went on duty that night and, as I worked, everything I had seen and heard over the last few months kept turning over and over in my mind. I tried to concentrate on what I was doing, but no matter where I turned, I kept thinking about God, and I could not get these thoughts out of my head. At the end of the evening when the rest of the staff went home, I sat alone in the kitchen and could hear the family singing choruses in their sitting-room. I sat and listened for a while and then I said, 'God, why can't I be like that? What is stopping me from being like that?' In that instant the reply came so plain and clear: there was nothing to stop me being like that; the only thing that was stopping me was myself; the very life I was leading was a total rejection of Jesus Christ. For seventeen years I had called myself a Christian; yet I had never once acknowledged Christ, and my lifestyle was far from the standards of Christ.

I went back to my room after that and did something I had never done before—I picked up a Bible and started reading. I also read more of the book *Joni* that had been given to me earlier in the evening. After a time, I just lay back in my bed and spoke to God. By this time it was well into the small hours of the morning, and I quite simply talked to God and poured out my seventeen years of existence to Him. And I choose my words carefully when I say 'existence,' because that's what these years were. I was seventeen and I felt I had merely existed, going from day to day, month to month, year to year, without really living. I told God how I felt inside, I told Him why I had come to Skye in the first place, really hoping to change, but that my life seemed worse than before I left Glasgow. As I spoke to Him, a really lovely thing happened: the atmosphere in the room actually changed. Where there had been a coldness, a 'nothingness' before, there actually came a warmth into the atmosphere. I could not have told you what it was at the time, but I now know it was the Presence of God coming into that room. So real and moving was it, that I just slipped out of my bed and got down on my knees before God and said, 'God, change me, make me a better person.' I didn't know how God was going to do this, but I knew that I really did need changed. I remember saying, 'God, I know you can hear me and I know you're going to answer me,' and there was a real sense of happiness within me. Tears of joy were flowing down my cheeks and I knew for the first time in my life that I could truly, truly call myself a Christian.

The following day, the reality of what had happened was still very much with me, but there was one thing which concerned me. I could just imagine going home and telling my family that I had really become a Christian, and being met with very real disapproval. So, again I spoke to God. I said, 'God, I know what has happened is real, but could you just do something to show me that I am on the right road?'—within a week of uttering those words, that prayer was wonderfully answered. One morning, after I had been working in the dining room of the hotel, one of the hotel guests called me over and asked me to sit down. I was quite taken aback because in the months of my being there, not one of the many, many guests had approached me in this way. I reluctantly sat down, and what followed was incredible. The lady was an elderly missionary who had been staying in the hotel for about a week, and her words to me were as follows: 'I've been watching you, and you look to me as if you are a good Christian girl; I would like to give you these two booklets to help you to help others.' This amazed me. I had never been referred to as a Christian before and the word 'good' as applied to me felt most strange! It had never been used before! The lady went on to tell me of a time in her life when she had been feeling really low. A situation had arisen and she didn't know what to do about it. She told me that as she lay in her bed one night God spoke to her and said, 'I will never leave thee nor forsake thee.' She said, 'That night, I slept like a baby.' As she spoke to me, I remembered how I had asked God less than a week previously if He would do something to show me I was on the right road, and I was in no doubt whatever that this was God answering my prayer. Nobody had bothered to speak to me about Christ before, and here was an old lady calling me over to her in the middle of a hotel dining room and speaking to me about God—this was no mere coincidence, this was the hand of God at work. The lady, before speaking to me, had no idea of the commitment I had made just days earlier and there was an obvious joy when I told her what had happened.

Later on that same day, I went to see my sister Pauline, who was working a few miles away. I told her what had happened to me and showed her the booklets I had been given in the morning. Over the months I had been telling her about the 'religious happenings' in the hotel. I was very enthusiastic about my recent experience. She sat in silence while I spoke and I later discovered that her first reaction was simply: 'They've *got* to her.'

Three weeks later, I returned to Glasgow and I was determined that this was not going to be a flash in the pan experience—it had been too real for that. I wanted to go on and find more of God. The first thing I did when I came home was buy a Bible, the first Bible to be in our home. Having been brought up in the Catholic Church, we were never discouraged from reading the Bible, but neither were we encouraged to read it, and so my knowledge of the Bible was very limited. As I started to read, whole passages seemed to live and I felt as if God was speaking directly to me; it was almost as if the words had been written with me in mind. One verse which particularly spoke to me was from Matthew 6:34: 'Therefore, do not worry about tomorrow, for tomorrow will worry about its own thing. Sufficient for the day is its own trouble.' My life previous to becoming a Christian was one of constant worry. I would worry about everything and worry about nothing. I would lie in my bed at night and just worry, worry, worry. Then one day soon after my salvation I read those words and I can honestly say that to this day I have been free from worry. Yes, there can be a natural and right concern for various situations, but there is a real difference between concern and *worry*, and for me the latter became a thing of my unsaved days. What a relief to know that we do not have to go through life worrying.

12

A Deepening Work

Three weeks after returning home and asking God to show me what to do, my sister started teacher training at Jordanhill College. There by seeming coincidence she met a Christian girl who invited us along to a meeting. I was very keen to go, thinking it was a Youth Fellowship gathering of a type to which I had been a couple of years previously. However, very shortly after walking through the doors of Struthers Memorial Church in Glasgow, I realised that this was no normal Y.F. meeting. When the minister opened in prayer, I heard others around me begin to speak quietly in an undertone. Then I heard of an experience known as the Baptism in the Holy Spirit and that, as on the day of Pentecost when the hundred and twenty in the upper room were filled with the Holy Spirit and began to speak in tongues, so also does this same experience still happen today. I then realised that the quiet speaking I had heard when Mr Black opened in prayer was speaking in tongues. I had never in my life heard of this happening today and I must admit there was a part in me which was really, really afraid. Here I was, in a church I had never been in before, with people I had never met before, and by way of introduction I was listening to them speaking in different languages which they said were given to them by God. So, yes, a part of me was very much afraid, but there was also a part of me which felt, 'I really want this.'

I have discovered a principle which operates time and time again—simply that one's spirit responds to truth. I may hear something which at a mind level seems very difficult to comprehend or accept, but I have found that in such cases, if truth is being imparted to me my spirit responds to it. That is exactly what happened to me when I heard for the first time about the Baptism in the Spirit. It was difficult to accept it at a mind level, but my spirit picked up the truth of it. After we had heard testimonies as to how some of the people there had received the experience, Mr Black asked if I wanted to be prayed with. Although there was one part in me which was afraid, another part was keen and I said, 'Yes.' That very same night, I too was baptised in the Holy Spirit and began to speak in new tongues, in a language I had never heard before. It wasn't French, it wasn't German, it wasn't any language I had ever learned; I could not have translated word for word what I was saying, but one thing I knew, and that was that I was praising God in a way I had never been able to do before and there was a feeling that it was reaching the very throne of God Himself.

When hearing of the way other people have received their Baptisms, I have noticed that some are hallmarked by love, others by a sense of joy, others by a sense of nearness of Christ. I found that my Baptism was hallmarked by peace. On the night I was baptised in the Holy Spirit, the peace of Christ came absolutely flooding over my being, a peace that until that point I never knew existed. In Scripture, we read of 'the peace of God which passeth all understanding,' and that very same peace filled me to overflowing. Peace was a quality which was markedly lacking in my life and it is something I hold very, very precious. I know what it's like to live without that peace and I now know what it's like to have it daily in my life, and I value it very highly indeed.

13

The Outcome

My salvation and Baptism took place in 1978, and much has happened in the intervening period. I found that as my desire for God grew, so the desire for pubs and dances lessened, until the latter disappeared. I wanted God, and therefore I went to the places where I knew I would find Him and I hadn't found Him in the pubs and dance halls. For a time after my salvation and Baptism I attended both the Catholic Church and the Pentecostal church, but there came a point when I felt God wanted me to join the latter. From the time of my becoming a Christian until the day I left the Catholic Church, there were very many and varied opportunities to speak to both clergy and laiety about my own experience and the reality of God in my life. Mr Black was very, very wise and left me to discover truth for myself. As I read the Bible, God Himself revealed truth to me and I accepted and embraced it wholeheartedly with a real desire that those I left behind who did not know that truth would come to know it too.[1]

I have known the very real direction of God in many different situations and I believe in seeking His will in all aspects and areas of life. Life has by no means been easy—we are never promised a bed of roses when we hand our lives over to God; there have been times of real testing, of real sorrow, but throughout it all I can testify to the utter faithfulness of Christ. The words spoken to me the week after my salvation, 'I will never leave thee nor forsake thee,' have proved true to the letter.

In his introduction, Mr Black mentions that Pauline and I are involved in deliverance ministry, and he has asked me to say a little about the visual side of this. From the beginning of this operating in me, I noticed that I had clear visual revelation of what was happening within people being set free.[2] The pictures are wonderfully varied. The last case in which I was involved, along with others, was no later than this week, and will serve as a good illustration. A man was in desperate need: he had known God in earlier days but had backslidden very badly. God had brought him back, but during his time away an evil power had entered. He had a spirit of violence. Indeed in his time away he almost killed a man. As a group of us ministered to him, the violence erupted and strong hands were required to hold him down. I could clearly see a spiral of darkness, something like a swirling tornado, within him. Suddenly there seemed to be an explosion of power within Mr Black, and the darkness was fragmented as God moved in power. In a moment of time, the man was delivered.

In another case with which we dealt recently, the person concerned had been involved in occult practices prior to his salvation. As we began to pray, it became apparent to me that there was within him something like a thick sea of mud, and within this there was intense movement and flailing around. As we continued, the thick mass of mud was brought right up to the surface and expelled.

In a still earlier case a young man came for ministry who was a very fine person, and he genuinely was following Christ. But things from his life prior to salvation still bound him, although he struggled against them. He was wonderfully released, and as this took place I saw as it were a wind blowing through him and sweeping away all the clouds of difficulty. A deep peace then followed.

Evil entities within people manifest themselves in many different forms, as in these cases. At times there can be revelation of an entity which is hiding quietly, lying low, while other entities are being driven out. There may come to me a very strong sense of the entity's thinking, 'If I hide here quietly, then when the noise has died down they will think that everything has gone, and I won't be noticed.' But I always feel it is a glorious moment when it realises that it has been discerned and is compelled to flee: it just cannot stay.

In closing, I would like to say that I don't regard what I have said as being 'my' testimony. I feel very much that this is simply a testimony to the grace and faithfulness and power of God. In my ten years of being a Christian, never once have I felt abandoned, never once have I felt let down, but time after time I have felt the warmth and the love of a Father in Heaven Who is closer to me than I would ever have imagined possible. To Him be all the glory.

Notes

[1] [*Author:* It is recognised, of course, that many Catholics now know the experience of the new birth and indeed many too are baptised in the Holy Spirit.]

[2] Perhaps I should mention that before the ministry began, I found that I could be in a meeting where others were ministering and have an accurate knowledge of what was happening within those who were being dealt with. This was never something that I imagined. It came as clear-cut revelation and knowledge and it happened although I was not myself involved in ministering in any direct way.

PAULINE

14

Finding Christ

As I write this, I am sitting in a Glasgow hospital at the bedside of my mother. She has been here for two months and is suffering from a number of complications which have arisen as a result of cancer. She may have only days—if not hours—to live. Thankfully, she knows Christ as her Saviour and there is no sense of distress or fear around this bedside. There is a quiet sense of peace as the Presence of God fills the room.

My parents were both Roman Catholics, and so I was taken along to mass every Sunday from as far back as I remember. I also went to confession every second Saturday evening and to mass on holidays of obligation and attended the forty hours adoration when it occurred. Catholicism was not just a ritual carried out on Sundays—it was a way of life. One of my earliest memories of religion concerned a Protestant friend who lived across the road from me. I remember clearly thinking what a pity it was that she would not go to Heaven when she died. I thought that Heaven was populated exclusively by Catholics!

Although I went to mass with unfailing regularity I was not a deep thinker about the things of God. I said my prayers every night but God always seemed very remote and it never occurred to me that we could individually experience a personal relationship with Him. If anyone had asked me if I believed in God, I would have emphatically said, 'Yes, of course,' but deep down inside, if the truth was known, I honestly did not know if He existed. I sincerely *hoped* He did and I thought that if a person lived a fairly good life he would go to Heaven. But all this was based on hope rather than faith. I have discovered that many other people share the view I once had—it was by no means unusual. They hope that God really does exist and that all will be well for them in the end.

In 1978, when I was seventeen years old, I left Glasgow for two months to work in a hotel in Portree on the Isle of Skye. My twin, Susie, had already been working in Skye for some time in another hotel some miles north of Portree.

She told me that her employers were Christians, but this term did not mean anything to me. So far as I was concerned they were Protestants and the term 'Christian' was meaningless. 'After all,' I thought, 'I am a Christian too.' However, from what Susie told me, these Christians were certainly more enthusiastic about their faith than I was. Jesus Christ seemed to mean a lot more to them than He did to me. I treated all these things which Susie told me very light-heartedly—even quite disrespectfully at times, I am sorry to admit!

At this point in Skye, my social life was everything I had hoped for. Night after night after night I enjoyed the round of the pubs and the dances on the island. The bright lights of Glasgow and the social life on Skye so dazzled my eyes that I had a wonderful time—or so it seemed at the time. I was really convinced that to be happy in this life you had to get out and immerse yourself in the social scene, and all would be well.

Then one afternoon Susie came to my room where I stayed in the hotel. To my great surprise she told me that having watched and listened to the Christians for whom she worked, she too had found Christ and really become a Christian. I listened intrigued as she told me of her experiences over the weeks and I had to admit to myself that I really would love to know for certain that God existed. I decided that I would start to find out Christian truths for myself. I was also a little worried about how my parents would react to this because, so far as we were concerned, Catholics didn't need to become Christians—all Catholics *were* Christians!

In October of that same year I returned to Glasgow to start teacher training at Jordanhill College of Education. In my first class I met a fellow student, Diana, through whom I really found Christ. After discovering that she was a Christian, I became friendly with her and two weeks later she invited Susie and me along to her church to a small youth meeting held on Tuesday nights. Unknown to me at that time, my life was never going to be the same again after that meeting.

The church to which my friend belonged was Pentecostal. This name meant nothing to me. I went to St Andrew's Church, so I just thought that 'Pentecostal' was the name of her church rather than a type of church.

Including Susie and myself, there were only six or seven people present at the meeting that night. Mr Black led the meeting and two or three people told how they had found Christ as their Saviour and had later received the Baptism in the Holy Spirit. Each said that on receiving the Baptism in the Holy Spirit they 'spoke in tongues.' This amazed me. I knew that almost two thousand years ago on the day of Pentecost the early disciples had spoken in tongues, but I thought that this was an isolated case, never having handled a Bible myself. I did not know that this was experienced by other Christians in the Book of Acts and it never occurred to me even momentarily that people could actually be baptised in the Holy Spirit and speak in tongues today. I then reasoned that if this experience happened two thousand years ago and still happened today, God *must* be real. To strengthen my conviction, Susie was prayed with that same night and received the Baptism in front of my own eyes. Now I didn't know anyone who was at that meeting that night except my new friend Diana, and it might have been possible that the people were fabricating what they said about this Baptism (although I knew they weren't) and they might have been making up strange sounds (although again I really knew they weren't). But of one thing I was sure. Something real had happened to my twin. I could not deny that she was speaking fluently in tongues. There was no doubt about it. I did not know these other people, but I did know Susie and there was no way she could speak as she was doing by herself.

That night my own Christian life began. My understanding of salvation was very limited but since I was convinced from what I saw and heard that night that God was real, I wanted Him to come into my life. At that stage I should have begun to change. I would like to testify that I was now aware of sin in my life and that I began to start life afresh, put away sinful ways and live completely for Christ. But it did not happen that way. In reality, there was a large part of my life which remained completely untouched by God. As the old illustration pictures it, I allowed Christ in the front door of my house but largely confined Him to one or two rooms only. Most of the rooms were closed to Him. I believe that many people are willing to accept Christ as Saviour but the number who want to accept Him as Lord—Lord over every part of their life—is more limited.

The main reason for my less than total commitment to Christ was my social life. I saw that the other Christians in this Pentecostal church did not have the same social life as myself—in fact, they didn't have any social life at all so far as I could see! I loved to go to a particular dance-hall on a Friday night—they went to church! I went to the lounge-bar in my local hotel on a Sunday night—they went to church! I sat down in front of the television during the week—they went to church! I could not imagine life without all my various forms of entertainment. Some Christians reading this will be shocked—and quite understandably—that I could have called myself a Christian at this point—but there was a part of me which truly did desire God in spite of my love for the world.

'So what,' you may ask, 'changed all that?'

15

A Changed Life

For four months a battle went on inside me. I did want to be a Christian but I found it virtually impossible to live the life God expects of us. Then one night, very suddenly, I was baptised in the Holy Spirit and the battle ceased. I was again at a meeting and the company turned to prayer. Suddenly I became aware of God in a way I had never experienced before—but He was very, very far away from me (looking back now I realise that it was not so much God Who was far away from me, but I who was far away from God). For the first time in my life I really wanted to be where He was. I wanted this more than I wanted anything else in the whole world. I wanted to reach Him so much that I shouted, 'Oh, God!' I then felt myself being lifted, higher and higher. All the things which had once seemed so important to me were coming before me but I just pushed them away because there was only one thing which really mattered and that was to be where God was. Nothing else mattered. I was willing to give up my social life and all that went with it, and anything else which would hinder me from reaching God. A point was then reached where everything seemed to stop. My body had been shaking greatly as the power of the Holy Spirit had been pouring down upon me, taking me nearer and nearer to God. But then everything stopped. I was slightly puzzled. I did not feel that things were complete. I had no idea what should happen next but I said to God, 'You can't leave me here.' Instinctively I sensed there was something else still to happen. Within seconds of time, without my even thinking about it, new tongues were pouring out of my mouth. The power which had been falling upon me and welling up inside was now overflowing. The praise just flowed and flowed and flowed. I did not want to stop. Gradually I felt myself coming back down to earth again—and I was really disappointed! I would have been content to stay in that other realm forever. I am not exaggerating when I say I would have been glad if God had allowed me to stay there for the rest of my life and not brought me back at all. Never had I experienced anything so completely satisfying as that was.

I did not consciously think that life would change for me from that point on, but as I went back out into the world things were different. The social life and 'fun' which went with it ended. I could no longer go back to the places I had once enjoyed so much and thought I needed for survival. Since being baptised in the Holy Spirit, I could sense the uncleanness of these places. They were not places I would have wanted to take Christ to and as a follower of Christ there was no longer the desire to go there myself. The bright lights of social life which so dazzled my eyes had gone out and a new light was now shining for me.

Another result of the Baptism in the Holy Spirit was that I now wanted to tell other people about Christ. Previously I had dreaded anyone asking me if I was a Christian. I knew virtually nothing about the Bible and I did not know what I would say to people if they asked questions about my new faith. Now all that was changed. I was still only beginning to learn about the Bible, but the Baptism brought with it a power to witness for Christ. Within three days of receiving this experience I spent three hours talking to two of my friends about the reality of God and the joy He brought me. One of these friends became a Christian too a short time later and was baptised in the Holy Spirit.

As the months passed I found other changes taking place as God gained more and more control of my life. No longer did I feel free to decide how I would spend my holidays from college—God always indicated how these were to be spent. I remember clearly the first time this was put into practice. Just before my Baptism I had decided to return to Skye the following summer to work for four months in the hotel where I had been in the preceding summer. The job was arranged, my employers were expecting me—then after my Baptism God spoke. He showed me clearly that He wanted me to remain in Glasgow for the summer, continue to attend the Pentecostal church and deepen in my Christian life. Looking back now I realise how fatal it would have been to cut my ties with Christians at that early point in my experience. As it happened, had I not obeyed the voice of God, it might have been physically fatal as well as spiritually. I took suddenly ill with acute appendicitis, and the position I would have been in in Skye really could have endangered my life—because of the need of urgent, specialised medical attention. Indeed, I would probably not have sought medical help in Skye, since I thought my pains were similar to those experienced on earlier occasions. It was my parents who insisted on it at home. This principle of constantly seeking God's guidance in every area of life has continued since then. I truly believe that the verse which says, 'In *all* thy ways acknowledge Him and He shall direct thy paths,' should be strictly adhered to and practically outworked in our day to day Christian living. I have found that God has clearly and faithfully shown how my spare time and holidays should be spent. He is with me in my friendships, at my work and indeed in every aspect of life. Regarding friendships, I should say that prior to my Baptism I felt free to have friendships of my own choosing with members of the opposite sex, as young people do. In coming into this new relationship with God, that immediately ended. I have felt very clearly that for a Christian, first, a close relationship with a boy should be serious and never casual, and second, it should not be entered into unless it is clearly given by God. In my own case, this meant ending a relationship which I had formed before being baptised in the Spirit. I am aware that this is not how the world generally lives—nor even a large part of the Christian world—but it seems to me to be the only way which conforms to the teachings of Christ.

There was one other particular experience which occurred about eighteen months after my Baptism in the Spirit which had a profound effect on my spiritual development. I truly wanted to fulfil whatever God's will was for my life. I had (and still have) an extremely sensitive conscience and I could not deliberately have taken a known wrong road and tried to cover it up and deceive myself. My conscience could never have allowed that. At my deepest level I wanted to know God and to have Him Lord over my life. Then, at a church summer camp meeting in 1980, as we turned to prayer I found it impossible to reach God. I did not sense that He was far away as I did at the initial stages of my Baptism in the Holy Spirit—I just could not reach Him. It was as though there was an invisible barrier—something intangible holding me back. This alarmed me. I had never experienced anything like this before.

Before leaving the meeting I spoke to Mr Black and we turned to prayer. Things happened very swiftly. Immediately I felt as though I was in an underground tunnel. It was sloping upwards fairly gently in front of me. On the left hand side Christ was standing. It was not His physical appearance which struck me—it was what He *is*. He was completely unafraid and undaunted by any barrier within me. There was a strength in Him which cannot be imagined with the human mind. In my own mind I see it as 'absolute strength.' There is no human or evil power which can be compared to the power of Christ. He is completely unbending. (I find it very difficult actually to find words which accurately convey what I felt and saw—it is something very, very real but cannot easily be transmitted by words. There are those, however, who will well understand the depth of power and fearlessness which I am trying to describe.)

That power in Christ came against the barrier within me and I had a moment of choice. Either I could keep the barrier or side with Christ against it. I chose Christ and immediately I felt as though I was propelled up the tunnel at tremendous speed. The barrier could not remain in the presence of Christ. In moments it was gone and has never returned.

Shortly afterwards I found that there was power to make deeper inner decisions in dedicating my life to Christ which I could never have done prior to this experience. I believe that had Christ not stepped in at that point and dealt with that invisible barrier, there were deep decisions concerning sanctification which I would never have been able to make, not even to this day. I would not intentionally have backslidden, but it would have been impossible to make further unhampered progress in Christ.

16

Working for God

Although the experience described at the end of the last chapter happened over eight years ago, it has had particular relevance over recent months. Some time ago Mr Black prayed with me at the end of a meeting. I felt my spirit soaring upwards, as it were into the sky. There was nothing to hold me to earth—no barriers, no bondages—just perfect freedom. If you can picture an eagle flying high in a clear sky, soaring with ease and freedom in the vast expanses of an open heaven, that is how I felt. I was totally free, like a bird on the wing.

In the days following this experience I found a new strength and power within me as I prayed. It was the same power which I had known in Christ over eight years previously, when He had been liberating me. At that time He was standing outside me in one sense, but now that power was right inside me.

When I told Mr Black about what had happened, he indicated that he believed this had come for a reason—so that others could be set free through the ministry of deliverance. Since then, there has been opportunity to pray with many who have needed to be set free from bondages of many kinds—some of long standing. I rejoice that one after another Christ has met them and set them free. Sometimes it has been really glorious. To see people delivered from fear, as we do again and again, brings tremendous joy. One such case was of a lady who was full of bitterness and resentment due to past injuries. She repented of her attitude and immediately was wonderfully delivered and then baptised in the Spirit.

Others have been delivered from lust, uncleanness, past unhealed hurts, and effects of occult influences. The cases are too numerous to detail, but perhaps one other could be included. During the course of a service one young man was at first very responsive. Then, when deliverance was presented, his head went down and God wonderfully dealt with him. Before even coming for private ministry a bondage broke like a chain snapping from his neck. When he was a child his father had tightened a lasso round his neck, and ever after a fear and bondage remained. He was totally delivered.

To see joy replace unhappiness and strength and courage flow into lives that have been broken and bound gives joy unspeakable to those who are privileged to minister. My heart overflows with thankfulness to God for all He has done and for the entrance He has given into this realm. From the moment this ministry began to operate, it was like stepping into two new worlds—one of which I had not dreamed existed. I did know about God and something about His power—but I did not know or suspect the extent or depth of human need. It may be that we live in particularly evil times—but I have been shocked again and again at the depth of the pain and bondage in the lives of so many people, and previously I would never have had any inkling of this. These things seem to have been pushed down into the subconscious where they have festered sometimes for years. As these people receive ministry, not only is there joy at their release, but I know real anger at the cruelty of Satan in the lives of men. While rejoicing at the action of God, again and again I feel that if so many people within the churches are in such need what must it be like in the world, where sin is often unrestrained? By no means does one become complacent. The deeper you go into this ministry the more deeply is the need revealed. From a condition of comparative unknowing I have become aware of a situation which can only be described as horrendous and of which, as far as I have perceived it, the Church at large knows almost nothing. To so many people the emphasis in the ministry of Jesus on 'binding the strong man before destroying his goods' passes almost unnoticed. The fact that again and again He cast out demons seems to fade into the background as being something difficult to understand—but it was real, fearfully real. I wonder if people think that when Jesus went back to Heaven demons suddenly ceased to exist, or that the work of Satan stopped? I now deeply realise in working with people, that men and women are in as great need today as they were in New Testament times. The work of the devil has gone on and God expects the work of His servants also to go on. 'Greater works,' He once said, 'than these shall ye do.' He equipped His early servants like Paul in the ministry of deliverance and He is equipping an increasing number in this way today. 'When wickedness comes in like a flood, the Spirit of the Lord lifts up a standard against him.' I would like those who read this to know that the evil is widespread—much more so than is generally recognised—and the remedy, the operation of the mighty power of God, is available. Praise His holy Name.

I have noticed too that God has opened up new situations where preaching is concerned. Through the years, from time to time I have been asked to testify to what He has done in my life, but more recently I felt led to go regularly to pray and have fellowship with a lady whose movements were restricted. Soon a house group formed and preaching was necessary in this developing situation. In earlier times I had been involved in preaching regularly at informal youth gatherings. More recently I have felt a draw further afield and again this involves preaching. But I thank God that He does not call without equipping and I find that He gives clear guidance in what to do and His word for preaching comes quite clearly and unmistakably.[1] He has gone with me every step of the way.

No doubt there will be those reading this who will wonder how my parents, who were Catholics, reacted to my new interest and obvious commitment to the things of God.

At first they thought it was a 'phase' I was going through and would soon grow out of (incidentally, I had gone through many 'phases' prior to this and sooner or later outgrown them). As the months, and then years, began to pass and my commitment to God was obviously deepening rather than abating, they realised it was not a phase. They were very reasonable, however, and although I was attending a non-Catholic church they were sensible enough to admit that it had done me no harm—in fact quite the opposite.

As time passed I felt my ties with the Catholic Church loosening. Then two years after my salvation I felt God speak to me quite clearly and tell me to affiliate myself with the Pentecostal church and work for Him from that base. Although my parents were not overjoyed, they did not stand in my way because they admitted that it was nothing harmful with which I was involved. My father, in fact, during a short illness with cancer, came to the point of accepting Christ personally as his Saviour, just days before he died. I will never forget the awesome presence of God which filled our house during those days just prior to his death. There was a peace which was almost tangible. As we moved around the house, we all talked in whispers, being very careful not to disturb the deep, holy presence which hung mightily all around us. And now my mother lies in the same condition. That same peace is here also. She too accepted Christ into her life some time ago.

The prospect of death is very sobering, particularly when it happens to people who are very close to you. Apart from the pain of the personal loss, there is the awesome knowledge that they are going to a place from which there is no return, and suddenly it is borne in upon you that you too will go alone through the same experience. Earth life truly begins to fade away, and many things which were once so important pale into relative insignificance. Over my spirit there has come a deep seriousness and knowledge of how important spiritual things really are. As the Bible says, 'For what doth it profit a man, to gain the whole world, and forfeit his soul? For what should a man give in exchange for his soul?' These words are more real to me now than they have ever been.

In the affairs of this natural life, such as weddings or birthdays, an astonishing amount of time is often spent on preparation for the event. Months, and sometimes even years, can go into this—planning, organising and arranging, before people are satisfied that everything possible has been done that can be done to ensure success.

If so much care is taken in preparing for natural events, how much more careful ought we to be in preparing for spiritual events? Surely the rebirth is much more important than natural birth, and above all earthly things, we should prepare ourselves for our meeting with God. Surely our whole lives should be lived in the light of that day. May I close with the words of McCheyne, which are often quoted in our church: 'Eternity, eternity! Oh, let us live in the light of eternity! Let us live today as though we should never see tomorrow!'

I thank God for the day I met Christ, and I thank God that all my close family have found Him too.

Notes

[1] Since writing this testimony, Mr Black has asked me to include a recent experience which has affected me greatly. One Thursday morning in the middle of December, very shortly after my mother's death, the words of a Christian song began to run through my mind. The words were these:

> As I have been with you throughout the year
> I'll go before you, so have no fear.

All that day there was the feeling that God Himself was speaking to me in these words. The truth of them was alive and vibrant within me. On returning home from work, I began to read of the life of Joshua, and came across the promise given to him by God: 'As I was with Moses, so I will be with thee' (Joshua 1:5). As I was reading this, God spoke to me again, and the words, 'So I will be with thee,' came to me with all the force of an absolute promise which could not be broken. I knew they came from God Himself. We were standing on the threshold of a New Year—only two weeks away—and God was pledging Himself to be with me and indeed with the others in my house meeting too, in the year which lay ahead.

I began to think on the awesomeness of the promise which Joshua had been given by God. I reflected on the life of Moses and recalled how time after time after time God had moved in real miracle in his life. I remembered his encounter with God at the burning bush, his various audiences with Pharaoh, the miraculous provision and intervention during forty years of wilderness wanderings, the awesome Mount Sinai experiences, and many others. I realised that had Joshua never been given any other promise from God except this one, 'As I was with Moses, so I will be with thee,' he still had all he ever needed to take him into and through the Promised Land.

That Thursday night, something happened within me that had never happened before. Many times I had known God speak to me from the Bible, and I had never doubted the Voice that sounded. But the conviction which was within me that night was awesome. I did not merely *believe* that God had spoken. I *knew* He had spoken. It was like a solid rock inside me. I knew it to be God's voice as surely as I knew that I existed. The next night a similar experience occurred. As I was praying for a particular area where God was moving, there came once again that absolute knowledge that this work had by no means been initiated by man, but by God Himself, and it was His will that it be followed through. That rocklike knowledge has been of vital importance in moving forward in this particular work. I thank Him from the deepest part of my being for what He has done.

[*Author:* I want to comment on this. To my mind this is something of tremendous significance and is something which is really little understood amongst Christians. It is an entrance to a world of power. It is the means whereby kingdoms are subdued, mountains removed, and the work of God gloriously accomplished. The experience here obviously came quite unexpectedly and spontaneously and is, in my view, of tremendous importance. In my next book, *Gospel Vignettes,* there is a similar reference to faith in relation to 'Diana,' which is equally striking and which had remarkable consequences. I recommend readers to note this and would also refer them to the two chapters on faith in *Reflections on the Gifts of the Spirit.* Faith is far from being the chancy thing some people imagine it to be. There is a *law* of faith and it is absolute in its outworking. It is a sure and potent weapon in the hands of the servants of God, and much to be desired.

The fact that the same type of experience has happened twice in this way to Pauline, indicates to me that a new and vital phase in her ministry is beginning. I find it difficult to emphasise sufficiently how important I consider this kind of faith to be. It is a force, in the war against evil, of incalculable worth. It really does move mountains and subdues nations. It is associated with the strongest force in all the universe. It is close to the throne of power.]

APPENDIX ONE

The Two Messiahs in Jewish Theology

The following material is taken from Arnold Fruchtenbaum, *Jesus Was a Jew* (Broadman Press, 1974), pp. 23–24.

Anyone who sets himself to the task of seeking to know what the Old Testament has to say about the coming of the Messiah soon finds himself involved with a seeming paradox. At times one even seems to be faced with an outright contradiction. For the Jewish prophets gave a two-fold picture of the Messiah who was to come.

On the one hand, the inquirer will find numerous predictions regarding the Messiah which portray him as one who is going to suffer humiliation, physical harm, and finally death in a violent manner. This death was stated by the Jewish prophets to be a substitutionary death for the sins of the Jewish people. On the other hand, he will find that the Jewish prophets also spoke of the Messiah coming as a conquering king who will destroy the enemies of Israel and set up the messianic kingdom of peace and prosperity.

This is the two-fold picture the prophets gave of the Messiah. For centuries past, during the formulation of the *Talmud*, our rabbis made serious studies of messianic prophecies. They came up with this conclusion: The prophets spoke of *two different Messiahs.* The Messiah who was to come, suffer and die was termed MESSIAH, THE SON OF JOSEPH.* The second Messiah who would then come following the first was termed MESSIAH, THE SON OF DAVID.* This one would raise the first Messiah back to life, and establish the messianic kingdom of peace on earth. That the Old Testament presents these two lines of messianic prophecy was something that all the early rabbis recognised. The Old Testament never clearly states that there will be two Messiahs. In fact, many of the paradoxical descriptions are found side by side in the same passages, in which it seems that only one person is meant. But for the early rabbis the two-Messiahs theory seemed to be the best answer.

For centuries Orthodox Judaism held the concept of two Messiahs. Since the Talmudic period, however, in the history of the Jewish people the Son of David alone was played up in the imaginations of Jewish hearts and minds. The other messianic figure Messiah, the Son of Joseph, the suffering one, was ignored. He was there in Jewish theology when needed to explain the suffering Messiah passages contained in the Old Testament. His existence provided an escape clause when thorny questions were raised. Otherwise this messianic figure was largely ignored. Today few Jews have heard of Him or know of His existence in Jewish theology of days gone by. The one that Jews today know of is the one who is to conquer: Messiah, the Son of David.

* Capitals added

APPENDIX TWO

The Significance of Messianic Prophecies: Further Material from McDowell[1]

In his *Evidence that Demands a Verdict*, Josh McDowell includes the following observation on Peter Stoner's work:

> H. Harold Hartzler, of the American Scientific Affiliation, Goshen College, in the foreword of Stoner's book writes: 'The manuscript for *Science Speaks* has been carefully reviewed by a committee of the American Scientific Affiliation members and by the Executive Council of the same group and has been found, in general, to be dependable and accurate in regard to the scientific material presented. The mathematical analysis included is based upon principles of probability which are thoroughly sound and Professor Stoner has applied these principles in a proper and 'convincing way' (McDowell, p. 167).

Chapter 1 of my own text quotes Stoner as saying, 'We find the chance that any one man fulfilled all 48 prophecies to be 1 in 10^{157}.' He continues:

This is really a large number and it represents an extremely small chance. Let us try to visualize it. The silver dollar, which we have been using, is entirely too large. We must select a smaller object. The electron is about as small an object as we know of. It is so small that it will take 2.5 times 10^{15} of them laid side by side to make a line, single file, one inch long. If we were going to count the electrons in this line one inch long, and counted 250 each minute, and if we counted day and night, it would take us 19,000,000 years to count just the one-inch line of electrons. If we had a cubic inch of these electrons and we tried to count them it would take us, counting steadily 250 each minute, 19,000,000 times 19,000,000 times 19,000,000 years or 6.9 times 10^{21} years.

With this introduction, let us go back to our chance of 1 in 10^{157}. Let us suppose that we are taking this number of electrons, marking one, and thoroughly stirring it into the whole mass, then blindfolding a man and letting him try to find the right one. What chance has he of finding the right one? What kind of a pile will this number of electrons make? They make an inconceivably large volume. Such is the chance of any one man fulfilling 48 prophecies (*ibid.*).

Readers may also be interested in the eight prophecies to which particular reference was made and their fulfilment[2]:

1. BORN AT BETHLEHEM

Prophecy: But as for you, Bethlehem Ephrathah, too little to be among the clans of Judah, from you One will go forth for Me to be ruler in Israel. His goings forth are from long ago, from the days of eternity (Mic 5:2).

Fulfilment: ...Jesus was born in Bethlehem of Judea.... (Mt 2:1).

2. PRECEDED BY MESSENGER

Prophecy: A voice is calling, 'Clear the way for the Lord in the wilderness; make smooth in the desert a highway for our God' (Is 40:3).

Fulfilment: John the Baptist came, preaching in the wilderness of Judea, saying, 'Repent, for the kingdom of heaven is at hand' (Mt 3:1,2).

3. HE WAS TO ENTER JERUSALEM ON DONKEY

Prophecy: Rejoice greatly, O daughter of Zion! Shout in triumph, O daughter of Jerusalem! Behold, your king is coming to you; He is just and endowed with salvation, humble, and mounted on a donkey, even on a colt, the foal of a donkey (Zech 9:9).

Fulfilment: And they brought it to Jesus, and they threw their garments on the colt, and put Jesus on it. And as He was going, they were spreading their garments in the road. And as He was now approaching, near the descent of the Mount of Olives... (Lk 19:35–37).

4. BETRAYED BY A FRIEND

Prophecy: Even my close friend, in whom I trusted, who ate my bread, has lifted up his heel against me (Ps 41:9).

Fulfilment: ...Judas Iscariot, the one who betrayed Him (Mt 10:4).

5. SOLD FOR 30 PIECES OF SILVER

Prophecy: And I said to them, 'If it is good in your sight, give me my wages; but if not, never mind!' So they weighed out thirty shekels of silver as my wages (Zech 11:12).

Fulfilment: 'What are you willing to give me to deliver Him up to you?' And they weighed out to him thirty pieces of silver (Mt 26:15).

6. MONEY TO BE THROWN IN GOD'S HOUSE AND PRICE GIVEN FOR POTTER'S FIELD

Prophecy: So I took the thirty shekels of silver and threw them to the potter in the house of the Lord (Zech 11:13).

Fulfilment: And he threw the pieces of silver into the sanctuary and departed.... And they counselled together and with the money bought the Potter's Field as a burial place for strangers (Mt 27:5,7).

7. DUMB BEFORE ACCUSERS

Prophecy: He was oppressed and He was afflicted, yet He did not open His mouth (Is 53:7).

Fulfilment: And while He was being accused by the chief priests and elders, He made no answer (Mt 27:12).

8. CRUCIFIED

Prophecy (a): They pierced my hands and my feet (Ps 22:16).

Fulfilment: And when they came to the place called the Skull, there they crucified Him (Lk 23:33).

Prophecy (b): ...because He poured out Himself to death, and was numbered with the transgressors (Is 53:12).

Fulfilment: At that time two robbers were crucified with Him, one on the right and one on the left (Mt 27:36).

I would like to draw attention to further remarkable prophecies amongst those listed by McDowell[3]:

9. SMITTEN AND SPIT UPON

Prophecy: I gave My back to those who strike Me, and My cheeks to those who pluck out the beard; I did not cover My face from humiliation and spitting (Is 50:6).

Fulfilment: Then they spat in His face and beat Him with their fists; and others slapped Him (Mt 26:67).

10. GARMENTS PARTED AND LOTS CAST

Prophecy: They divide my garments among them, and for my clothing they cast lots (Ps 22:18).

Fulfilment: The soldiers therefore, when they had crucified Jesus, took His outer garments and made four parts, a part to every soldier and also the tunic; now the tunic was seamless, woven in one piece. They said...'Let us not tear it, but cast lots for it, to decide whose it shall be' (Jn 19:23,24).

11. GALL AND VINEGAR OFFERED HIM

Prophecy: They also gave me gall for my food, and for my thirst they gave me vinegar to drink (Ps 69:21).

Fulfilment: They gave Him wine to drink mingled with gall; and after tasting it, He was unwilling to drink (Mt 27:34).

12. BONES NOT BROKEN

Prophecy: He keeps all his bones; not one of them is broken (Ps 34:20).

Fulfilment: But coming to Jesus, when they saw that He was already dead, they did not break His legs (Jn 19:33).

13. HIS SIDE PIERCED

Prophecy: They will look on Me whom they have pierced (Zech 12:10).

Fulfilment: But one of the soldiers pierced His side with a spear (Jn 19:34).

14. DARKNESS OVER THE LAND

Prophecy: 'And it will come about in that day,' declares the Lord God, 'that I shall make the sun go down at noon and make the earth dark in broad daylight' (Amos 8:9).

Fulfilment: Now from the sixth hour darkness fell upon all the land until the ninth hour (Mt 27:45).

15. BURIED IN RICH MAN'S TOMB

Prophecy: His grave was assigned to be with wicked men, yet with a rich man in His death... (Is 53:9).

Fulfilment: There came a rich man from Arimathea, named Joseph...and asked for the body of Jesus.... And Joseph took the body and wrapped it in a clean linen cloth, and laid it in his own new tomb... (Mt 27:57–60).

Notes

[1] See chap. 1.

[2] The following prophecies and their fulfilments are culled from Josh McDowell, *Evidence that Demands a Verdict*, pp. 149–61.

[3] *Ibid.*, pp. 160–66.

NOTE TO READERS

If you would like to enquire further about issues raised in this book or if you feel that the author could be of help, you are invited to write to him at 27 Denholm Street, Greenock, PA16 8RH, Scotland, or telephone 0475 87432.

It may also be of interest to know that the author is normally involved in five conferences in Scotland each year—New Year, Easter, July, August and October. Friends gather from many parts of Britain. An open invitation is extended to all and particularly to those interested in the Baptism in the Holy Spirit and related themes. Details will be provided on enquiry.

By the same author

Reflections on the Baptism in the Holy Spirit

The Baptism in the Holy Spirit...

- Is it something that happens to us all at conversion, or is it a later and separate experience?
- Should people tarry for it?
- Is it the same as sanctification?
- Do tongues always come with it?
- What about men like Spurgeon and Finney? Did they have this experience?

This book honestly faces many of the problems that the Baptism in the Spirit has raised in the minds of so many in our day. The fact that tens of millions of people now claim to have had this experience, which they describe as similar to what happened to the early disciples on the day of Pentecost, makes the book both topical and relevant.

Published in December 1987, the book has proved very popular and is being used to bring people into the experience of which it speaks.

£2.25 UK 128pp

By the same author

Reflections on the Gifts of the Spirit

This book speaks of...

- the wonderful operation of the gift of knowledge
- demon exorcism
- miracles of many kinds

Examples are largely drawn from the present day and fall within the personal experience of the author, or of people close to him. Intriguing questions are raised...

- Do demons still speak through human lips?
- Can people receive instantaneous healing?
- Is the future sometimes accurately revealed to God's servants?
- Is angelic ministry real and does it happen today?
- Finally does an ex-Headmaster of a large secondary school, qualified in History (a subject which so often breeds sceptics) believe all these things?

This book was published in March 1988 and contains a number of unusual insights on the gifts in general and on healing, miracles and exorcism in particular.

£2.75 192pp

By the same author

Reflections on a Song of Love

(A Commentary on 1 Corinthians 13)

First Corinthians Thirteen has a beauty which has enthralled readers through the ages. It highlights Love and reveals attributes of Christ Himself. It has, however, often been used by opponents of Pentecostal doctrine—quite wrongly, the author maintains. He raises intriguing questions...

- 'Whether there be tongues, they shall cease': did this happen with the close of the canon of Scripture?
- Did knowledge cease at the same time? Will knowledge ever cease in this life, and what will replace it in Heaven?
- When Paul became a man he 'put away childish things.' Did this not include tongues?
- Do Christians generally attain the level of Love taught here, and do they display it in their attitudes to each other, as, for example, when these doctrines deeply divide them?

While the main part of this book gives a wonderful description of Christ and the quality of His Love, these controversial issues are not overlooked. Published in April 1988, this highly original commentary on 1 Corinthians 13 has attracted considerable attention.

£1.25 64pp

By the same author

A Trumpet Call To Women

Is it true that in the Old Testament there were:

Prophetesses?
A Woman Judge?
A Queen (in her own right)?

and in the New Testament:

Prophetesses?	Women Apostles?
Women Teachers?	Women Elders?
Women Evangelists?	Women Deacons?

- What did Paul mean when He taught that in the Church there is neither male nor female?
- And was what the Maréchale said true, 'There is no sex in soul'?
- And are all the spiritual functions which are open to men equally open to women?
- Or should women be in a role subject to men?

This is a highly original piece of writing. The author deals in a Biblical way with the question of women ministry. Unlike those who base their case on 'cultural relativism', Mr Black finds his support in the writings of Paul himself. He produces what to many will be an unexpectedly powerful and persuasive case for the ministry of women.

This is a valuable contribution to the current debate.

Published in 1988, this thoughtful and original work has attracted wide attention.

£2.50 160pp

By the same author

Consider Him

(Twelve Qualities of Christ)

Like a man gazing into a fathomless pool the author has looked into the infinite deeps of Christ. As the colours of a glorious sky are reflected in ever changing light so the radiance of heaven is reflected in the soul of Christ. We see glory change to glory as we behold His face.

What are the qualities which appear as in a kaleidoscope?

- Peace and Serenity
- Purity and Tranquillity
- Love and Compassion
- Strength and Courage
- Self-effacement and God-centredness
- Power and Glory

The subjects are not treated in a milk and water way. At times the writing cuts like a knife and lays bare our very souls. Our loyalty and commitment are deeply challenged as we are measured, not by our own faulty standards but by His perfection; nor are we expected to stop at intellectual instruction. Change is demanded and expected.

In the second part of the book we see in Miss Jack's life the power of God to effect change. Through crucifixion of the self life and through pain, the Christ nature developed; this always makes for fascinating reading.

Published in 1988 this book should appeal to Christians interested in both sound doctrine and a devotional approach to God.

£2.25 128pp

By the same author

Battle for the Body

As in battle rival commanders aim for the same strategic points and seek to exploit each other's weaknesses so in the spiritual war, where the bodies of men are the battlefield, God and Satan aim to secure control of the same vital centres. Each is interested in areas of weakness—Satan that he may enter and destroy—God that He may guard and strengthen. Satan wants the body to be under his control, obeying his commands and ultimately being possessed by him. God wants the same body that it may be wholly His—a channel for His Spirit; holy, strong and pure.

What are the strategic points around which the battle rages?

- Head • Eyes • Ears • Tongue
- Shoulders • Heart • Knees • Backbone
- Hands • Feet • Reproductive Organs

You may be surprised at who really controls these parts of our bodies. Examine the evidence as it is revealed in this searching book.

The second part of the book tells of how battle was waged between God and Satan for one particular life. The story of Rev John Hamilton has thrilled thousands in Britain, Europe, India and America. It is a remarkable story.

Published in 1988 this book has a practical flavour which will appeal to many.

By the same author

The Clash of Tongues: with Glimpses of Revival

This book is divided into two sections. The first deals not only with the regulation of gifts of the Spirit and their relevance for today but also with some of the deeper principles underlying their use. It raises fundamental questions which are sometimes overlooked:

- How can an individual be edified through speaking something which neither he nor his hearers can understand?
- Is there a spiritual means of communication between the human spirit and God which by-passes the intellect but still yields benefit?
- Why did Paul have to make regulations at all? If the gifts are gifts of the Spirit, how can error creep into their use and may the regulations not clash with the direct unctioning of the Spirit upon an individual?
- Tongues, according to verse 2 of 1 Corinthians 14, are Godward. Why then is interpretation so often manward? Surely if God is addressed in one, He will be addressed in the other. Is there Scriptural justification for present-day practice and is there a difference between the tongues of Acts 2, which were understood by foreigners and the 'tongues' of 1 Corinthians 14 which 'no man' understood?

The second part of the book deals with the relationship between revival and Pentecost. It refers to the 1939 and 1949 revivals in Lewis—the first of which has been little publicised although it seems to have been more powerful than the second. A number of people who were much used in this are introduced and the main part of the story is centred on the life and experiences of Mary MacLean, now an old lady of 83, who had quite remarkable visions. Hers is a fascinating story.

An appendix of this book contains evidence that Finney, Moody and Spurgeon were all baptised in the Spirit and all spoke in tongues.

Published in 1988 this book, while of general interest, is expected to appeal particularly to serious students of the New Testament.

£2.75 191 pp

By the same author

Gospel Vignettes

This book focuses attention on various facets of the gospel. The chapter titles give the flavour:

- Ye Must Be Born Again
- The Life-Giving Water
- The Gospel on the Lips of Paul
- I Am Proud of the Gospel
- Weighed in the Balances of God
- When I See the Blood
- The Brazen Serpent
- The Broad and Narrow Ways
- The Lost Son
- The Lost Sheep
- The Lost Coin
- God So Loved
- Behold I Stand at the Door and Knock
- The Hour of Decision

It also includes the testimonies of three people whose lives have been transformed by Christ.

Due to be published early in 1989, this book should prove useful to all who are involved in spreading the gospel.

BOOK ORDERS

The books advertised on the previous pages are being made available to Christian booksellers throughout the country, but if you have any difficulty in obtaining your supply, you may order directly from New Dawn Books, c/o 27 Denholm Street, Greenock, Scotland, PA16 8RH.

.... ORDER FORM ....

Please send me the books indicated below:

Quantity	Title	Price
	Reflections on the Baptism in the Holy Spirit	£2.25
	Reflections on the Gifts of the Spirit	£2.75
	Reflections on a Song of Love (A commentary on 1 Cor 13)	£1.25
	A Trumpet Call to Women	£2.50
	Consider Him (Twelve Qualities of Christ)	£2.25
	Battle for the Body	£2.95
	The Clash of Tongues: with Glimpses of Revival	£2.75
	The Incomparable Christ	£2.75
	Gospel Vignettes	£2.75
	Reflections from Abraham	£2.25

Signature ....

Address ....

....

....

When ordering please send purchase price plus 30p per book to help cover the cost of postage and packaging.